‖‖‖ ‖ ‖‖‖‖‖‖ ‖ ‖‖ ‖ ‖‖ ‖‖‖‖‖‖‖‖‖‖‖‖‖ ‖‖
◁ **W9-AQO-075**

IT ALL DEPENDS

A comparison of situation ethics and
the Playboy philosophy with what the Bible
teaches about morality.

BY FRITZ RIDENOUR

Illustrated by Joyce Thimsen
Research by Georgiana Walker

A Division of G/L Publications
Glendale, California, USA

The publishers do not necessarily endorse the entire contents of all publications referred to in this book.

Scripture quoted from Living New Testament is copyrighted by Tyndale House Publishers, 1967 and is used by permission.

Quotations of more than 50 words from books and magazines are used by permission from the publishers.

Over 165,000 in print
Second Printing, 1969
Third Printing, 1969

©Copyright 1969 G/L Publications

Printed in U.S.A.

Published by
Regal Books Division, G/L Publications
Glendale, California, U.S.A.

Library of Congress Catalog Card No. 68-8388
SBN 8307-0040-4

Contents

A teaching and discussion guide for use with this book is available from your Sunday School supplier or your local Christian Bookstore.

Foreword

This is a book about morals, written essentially for Christians in the "under 25" generation. If you do not embrace the Christian faith or are "on the fence," we hope you will still take time to peruse the reasons given for the Biblical view of morality.

It All Depends makes a frank analysis of the view of two leading proponents of the new morality: Joseph Fletcher, author of *Situation Ethics,* and Hugh Hefner, editor-publisher of *Playboy* magazine and author of the "Playboy Philosophy." While these men do not share exactly the same views on sex and morals, both of them are highly articulate and write convincingly for their points of view.

There is little question that Joseph Fletcher and Hugh Hefner have had a great influence and impact on society. You may have never heard of Fletcher, or even Hefner (as popular as *Playboy* magazine is). You are, however, exposed daily to their ideas, viewpoints and beliefs.

All of us—Christian or not—face the sticky situations that Fletcher claims to solve with his situation ethics. All of us face the temptations of selling out to the hedonistic pursuit of pleasure that Hefner advocates each month.

A lot of people—particularly the younger generations—are buying the bill of goods called the "new morality." And, let us face it, a lot of these people have "grown up in the church." You may well be one of them.

It's not that you don't know the answers. You know that the Bible says, "No sex outside of marriage." But perhaps what is bothering you is *why* the Bible says this and what exactly are the real advantages of doing as the Bible teaches? In other words, why is it worth it to stay virgin until you are married when most of your friends seem so worldly wise, so "experienced" in the game of life?

These are valid questions. They can't be answered with simple pronouncements of righteous faith. Hefner and Fletcher appeal to the natural desire of any human personality—to be free, to be independent, to make decisions on its own. But they are wrong, and not simply "because the Bible says so." They are wrong because of one other basic characteristic of "being human." We demand our freedom, but we want guidance and help. We boast of our achievements, but we are morally blind, and in our candid rational moments, we know it.

All of us enjoy pleasure, but pleasure alone will never satisfy. As an ancient Roman philosopher said: "No man is free who is slave to flesh." Slavery to appetites—sexual and otherwise—offers no lasting satisfaction; neither does being captive to a long list of "do's and don'ts."

Most of us want to know: "How can I be really free? Religious legalism is no answer. Does the Bible really speak to the moral problems that I have to face?"

Read on. It all depends.

Fritz Ridenour
Youth Editor, Gospel Light Publications

CHAPTER 1

Is ~~MORALITY~~ making its last stand?

Is the human race suffering a complete breakdown in morals? A look at the recent record is not too encouraging.

In Amsterdam, Holland, prostitution is practiced under government license and jurisdiction, with girls displayed on sofas in brightly lighted store front windows.

In Copenhagen, Denmark, hard-core pornography picturing anything and everything, even the intimate details of homosexuality and lesbianism, is easily available at the corner newsstand.*

The church in Sweden is waging a losing, if not lost, battle against sexual liberalism. Premarital sex is practically a Swedish way of life. According to one survey in that country, two-thirds of the Swedish women are pregnant by their wedding day and

---

Hey Preach, You're Coming Through. David Wilkerson. Copyright 1968, Fleming H. Revell, p. 17 and following.

1

95 percent have begun their sexual life by the time they are married.*

But the "sex-happiest" country of them all has to be the United States where the battle cry of the sexual revolution is "anything goes." John Q. Public is bombarded with sex in every enticing shape and form, from TV commercials ("Take it off, take it *all* off") to "adult" and "mature" films that leave *nothing* to the imagination (*I, a Woman; The Penthouse; Who's Afraid of Virginia Woolf?;* etc., etc.).

Playboy magazine is the supposed "bible" of the college set. What used to be labeled hard-core pornography now sells openly on newsstand and paperback racks (*Candy, The Tropic of Cancer, The Exhibitionist,* etc., etc.).

More Babylonian than Babylon itself

Historian and newspaper columnist Max Lerner has said: "We're living in a Babylonian society, perhaps more Babylonian than Babylon itself.... The emphasis in our society today is on the senses and the release of the sensual. All the old codes have been broken down."**

Sex is not the only frontier where morality seems to be making its last stand.

According to the Uniform Crime Report of 1967, released by the United States attorney general and FBI director J. Edgar Hoover, more than 3,802,300 crimes were reported in the United States during 1967, a 16 percent increase over 1966. The 1930-

*"Swedish Church Vainly Battles Premarital Sex," Dan L. Thrapp, *Los Angeles Times*, Wednesday, July 17, 1968.
**"Anything Goes: Taboos in Twilight," *Newsweek*, November 13, 1967, p. 75.

page report reveals that there was one murder every 43 minutes, one forcible rape every 19 minutes, one robbery every two and a half minutes, one burglary every 20 seconds, one larceny ($50 and over) every 30 seconds, and one auto theft every 48 seconds.*

There is a touch of irony in the fact that a major campaign issue in the 1968 elections was not taxes, foreign aid or foreign policy, but "crime in the streets." Any number of America's large cities have experienced full-scale riots as people protest everything from the "unjust war" in Vietnam to the mistreatment of the Negro and minority races to the laws and traditions of the "establishment."

Even junior highers puff "magic dragon"

Drug use and addiction has increased throughout the 1960's until now the problem has reached into the junior high school level and even below.** Young people, in particular, find it hard to see why marijuana is outlawed when adults from another generation continue to imbibe freely from another addictive drug—alcohol.

And so it goes. The 60's have seen the decline, if not the fall, of the "old morality," and the "new morality" has risen to take its place. The "new morality" means different things to different people. Many limit the "new morality" to sexual misconduct. Actually the term "new morality" is used in a

*EP News Service, August 31, 1968.
**See "Children of the Drug Age," by sociologist-anthropologist William Simon and sociologist John N. Gagnon, *Saturday Review*, September 21, 1968, who point out that the use of marijuana among adolescents is no passing fad and will probably increase.

MANY PEOPLE LIMIT THE NEW MORALITY TO
THE SEXUAL REVOLUTION

narrow and inaccurate way if it is applied only to sex. Morality takes in the entire scope of a person's behavior. A person's morals are directly affected by his system of ethics, that is, his system of determining what is good or bad, right or wrong. The basic philosophy behind the new morality was not written by secular anarchists or publishers of hard-core pornography. Ironically enough, this philosophy has been developed by liberal and neo-orthodox theologians—men who claim loyalty to the Judeo-Christian traditions. A basic idea held by these thinkers is that the old laws and rules (meaning the Ten Commandments) are "out" and freedom and responsibility are "in."

Who's who in the new morality?

Perhaps the leading advocate of the new morality is Joseph Fletcher, former dean of St. Paul's Cathedral, Cincinnati, Ohio, now professor of social ethics at the Episcopal Theological School, Cambridge, Massachusetts. In 1966 Fletcher startled clergy and lay people alike with his book *Situation Ethics*, which spells out what Fletcher calls a "revolutionary approach to morals."*

Fletcher is a self-styled archenemy of what he calls "legalism." By legalism, Fletcher means recognizing a preset collection of rules and laws, such as the Ten Commandments, as authoritative for making decisions between right and wrong. Fletcher claims that you cannot possibly construct a once and for all code concerning right and wrong that is permanently binding on everyone in every situation. The only absolute authoritative law in Fletcher's system is what he calls the "law of love." In other words, the only thing that matters with Fletcher is "What is the loving thing?" not "What is legal."

Other advocates of the "new morality" include English theologian, Bishop John A. T. Robinson (author of *Honest to God*), who has pointed out that Christians in New Testament times set down their own system of ethics, but what was right for the first century isn't necessarily good for the 20th.**

In America, other advocates of the new morality

*From SITUATION ETHICS, by Joseph Fletcher. The Westminster Press. In British Empire: SCM Press Ltd. Copyright © 1966. W. L. Jenkins. Used by permission, p. 124.
***Christian Morals Today*, John A. T. Robinson. Copyright 1964, Westminster Press, p. 16.

I ask not how can I obey religious rules and traditions. Instead, I ask, is this right for me?

FOLLOWERS OF THE NEW MORALITY CLAIM A NEW SENSE OF PERSONAL FREEDOM

include the Right Reverend James A. Pike, former Bishop of the Episcopal Diocese of California and now on the staff of the Center for the Study of Democratic Institutions, Santa Barbara, California; Rabbi Richard L. Rubenstein, director of the B'nai B'rith Hillel Foundation and proponent of the "death of God" theological fad of the mid-1960's.

In a panel discussion sponsored by *Playboy* magazine in 1967, Rubenstein said, ". . . people are experiencing a sense of personal freedom. We now ask, 'Is this right for me?' we no longer ask, 'How do I comply with a set of inherited commandments from my religious tradition?' "*

To many people, these "new morality" viewpoints

Playboy, June 1967. "Playboy Panel: Religion and the New Morality."

sound quite "reasonable and responsible," even moral in their way. But at the base of what these men are saying is an attitude that recognizes no final authoritative guideline for life. "God's Word" is seen by advocates of the new morality as merely a collection of the moral traditions of mankind. In other words, say the new moralists, the Bible wasn't pronounced from on high and tossed down on golden tablets by some "big law-giver in the sky." The new moralists, rather, see the Bible as some kind of "code" written by men of another day who were far more qualified to talk about right and wrong in their own situation than in ours.

Private opinion or God's Word?

For example, when the apostle Paul wrote to the Corinthian church about its problems (dissension, incest, fornication, adultery, etc.) he was, say the new moralists, merely giving his own private opinions, not speaking the mind of God Himself.

But, would Christianity have survived in the first century Roman world if based only on private opinions and theories? Cities like Rome and Corinth were immersed in pagan polytheism and wholesale immorality. Roman philosophers such as Cicero, Seneca and Plutarch made a stab at suggesting that men honor their marriage vows, but they also cautioned wives not to be too hard on their men if they decided to stray a bit. Plutarch, for example, even offered the peculiar reasoning that a husband might have an affair with a prostitute out of respect to his wife.*

*How to Study 1 Corinthians, Joseph Gettys. Copyright 1951, John Knox Press, p. 57.

7

The world famous city of Corinth, located on the Aegean Sea in lower Greece, was a first century version of "sin-city" in every sense of the word. Corinth was internationally recognized as the most immoral (and therefore exciting) place that any man could ever visit. Sailors had a saying: "Not for every man is the trip to Corinth."

Corinth featured "red light religion"

Probably the outstanding attraction in Corinth was the Temple of Aphrodite, which was staffed by some 1,000 priestess prostitutes. Worship of Aphrodite, the goddess of fertility, included having sexual intercourse with one of these prostitutes. Naturally, many men living in Corinth or visiting there were quite faithful about carrying out their "religious duties."

Idolatry was common in the first century world. In Rome alone the people worshiped over a hundred pagan deities, and the Roman Christians were ironically tagged as atheists because they "did not worship the gods." But for all of their "religious ways," ancient inhabitants of cities like Rome and Corinth were actually hard-core secularists. Few of them actually believed in the many "gods" they worshiped. Reverence for pagan idols was simply part of being a Roman citizen. In this way, you showed your loyalty to the state and above all to Caesar who himself was worshiped as a "god."

The religion of the Roman Empire was really not a spiritual matter at all. It was a completely worldly, non-spiritual approach designed to let men do as they pleased with a clear conscience.*

*How to Study I Corinthians, Joseph Gettys, p. 11.

Citizens of first century Rome and Corinth had secular values. They not only failed to see beyond this life, they missed the real purpose of life, period. They devoted themselves to satisfying physical desires: hunger, thirst, sex, accumulating property, etc. What they could see and touch—the material—was all that mattered.

Into this world came Christianity, with the Gospel—the good news that God had broken into space and time in the person of Jesus Christ and had done something for the very souls of men. He had died for their sins and risen again from the dead as a guarantee that all who believed in Him would conquer death forever.

Seek the Kingdom, not a quick buck

The Christian Gospel turned the value system of the pagan world upside down. While not over-looking physical needs, Christianity taught men to seek first the Kingdom of God,* not a quick buck. Christianity didn't offer a short course in "how to reform." It offered people an opportunity to become brand new persons—to begin a new life.** The Gospel not only faced people with their sin; it asked them to change completely, to turn from their lust and self interest and live not for themselves but for God. Surrounded as it was by pagan immorality and idolatry, the Christian faith seemed doomed. All the odds were against Christianity, but it did not die. It grew and spread and finally overcame that pagan world by the sheer force of one basic argument:

*See Matt. 6:24-34.
**See II Cor. 5:17.

9

". . . We are telling you about what we ourselves have actually seen and heard, so that you may share the fellowship and the joys we have with the Father and with Jesus Christ His Son" (I John 1:3, *Living New Testament*).

Do men "come of age" need the Bible?

Through the centuries, the Bible has remained the "Magna Carta of morality"—guiding mankind to a right knowledge of God and providing a solid authority for knowing the difference between right and wrong.

But in the 20th century, the authority of Scripture is being seriously questioned by "men come of age"—the technologists of the secular city. Today's society is still basically secular, and more hung-up than ever on materialism because of the incredible scientific and technological strides made in the last 100 years.

Preachers of the "new morality" have come forward to replace what they call the "outdated" morality of the Bible. The new moralists label the Bible as some kind of legalistic code dreamed up by men who lived thousands of years ago, but who knew nothing about the problems, tensions, pressures, etc., faced by modern man who could destroy himself at the press of a button.

Are the new moralists right? It all depends—on several things: whether or not God is dead or alive; whether or not the Bible is a collection of human traditions or the Word of God revealed unto men; whether or not men have the ability to make "responsible judgments" and decisions on right and wrong without any help or wisdom that comes from

The Bible was good stuff in its day, but things are different now.

ARE PREACHERS OF THE NEW MORALITY RIGHT?
IT ALL DEPENDS . . .

above and beyond. And it all depends on just how "old and irrelevant" the Bible really is.

While there are many passages in the Scriptures that deal with the traditions and the events of Biblical times, there are many other passages like this:

"For people will love only themselves and their money; they will be proud and boastful, sneering at God, disobedient to their parents, ungrateful to them, and thoroughly bad. They will be hardhearted and never give in to others; they will be constant liars and troublemakers and will think nothing of immorality. They will be rough and cruel, and sneer at those who try to be good. They will betray their friends; they will be hot-headed, puffed up with pride, and prefer good times to worshiping God. They will go to church, yes, but they won't really believe anything they hear" (II Tim. 3:2-5, *Living New Testament*).

Are these words irrelevant to "men come of age" in the 20th century? On the contrary, they picture perfectly the moral condition of mankind today.

11

And yet, the new morality presents a clever and intelligently phrased argument for tossing out all rulebooks and living a life that is "meaningful and loving." This all sounds very noble, very intelligent, sophisticated, even convincing. While the advocates of the "new morality" may be sincere men who are honestly trying to seek a better approach to decisions between right and wrong, the terrible irony of the entire moral scene today is that the new morality and situation ethics have not proved to be the answer.

Instead of changing people from within and making them new towers of moral strength, the new morality has often been used as a tool of expediency by those who want to live as they please and love every minute of it. Offered as an answer to legalism, the new morality is often used as an excuse for lawlessness. This may not be the fault of the men who teach the new morality, but the facts are there—and the facts continue to pile up to a frightening conclusion: morality seems to be making its last stand.

In the following chapters you can take a closer look at the new morality and situation ethics as you think about questions like these:

Is the new morality really the answer for making decisions about right and wrong?

Is the new morality really something that helps you do what you are supposed to do, or is it a clever excuse for letting you decide to do what you really want to do?

Is morality really making its last stand?

Should Christians throw in the towel and join a

Since they've tossed out the rule book, I'll write my own.

THE "NEW MORALITY" IS A GREAT EXCUSE FOR LIVING AS YOU PLEASE AND LOVING EVERY MINUTE OF IT.

secular society that appears to be dashing to destruction?

The answers to these questions lie in the seemingly noncommittal phrase that titles this book: *It All Depends*. It all depends on your answer to one other crucial question: Is Biblical morality nothing more than trying to obey laws and rules from the Bible, or is Biblical morality based on a genuine life-changing relationship to Jesus Christ?

TAKE TIME . . .

Use the following ideas to take time to apply the Bible to your life and any situations you face.

Secular City versus the City of God

³"You should have as little desire for this world as a dead person does. Your real life is in heaven with Christ and God. ⁴And when Christ who is our real life comes back again, you will shine with Him and share in all His glories. ⁵Away then with sinful, earthly things; deaden the evil desires lurking within you; have nothing to do with sexual sin, impurity, lust and shameful

13

desires; don't worship the good things of this life, for that is idolatry" (Col. 3:3-5, *Living New Testament*).

What does it mean to "have no desire for this world"? What is the way to avoid being absorbed by secular thinking?

The rules of men or of God?

[1,2]"Let me add this, dear brothers: you already know how to please God in your daily living, for you know the commands we gave you from the Lord Jesus Himself. Now we beg you—yes, we demand of you in the name of the Lord Jesus—that you live more and more closely to that ideal. [3,4]For God wants you to be holy and pure, and to keep clear of all sexual sin so that each of you will marry in holiness and honor—[5]not in lustful passion as the heathen do, in their ignorance of God and His ways. [6]And this also is God's will: that you never cheat in this matter by taking another man's wife, because the Lord will punish you terribly for this, as we have solemnly told you before. [7]For God has not called us to be dirty-minded and full of lust, but to be holy and clean. [8]If anyone refuses to live by these rules he is not disobeying the rules of men but of God who gives His *Holy* Spirit to you" (I Thess. 4:1-8, *Living New Testament*).

Does this sound like legalism to you? Why? Why not? See especially v. 1 and v. 8.

For other examples of Biblical teachings on right and wrong see Gen. 13:5-18 (Abraham and Lot); I Sam. 24:1-15 (David and Saul); II Sam. 11, 12 (David and Bathsheba). Also review the Ten Commandments (Exod. 20:1-17).

TAKE INVENTORY . . .

If you are not a Christian, ask yourself these questions: Have I ever studied for myself what the Bible really teaches about Christ, Christianity and right and wrong? Have I confused Biblical morality with the "old morality" which is encrusted with church traditions and dogma? Do I think a person can be "good on his own" or does the record of experience, history, the current mess the world is in, and my own personal record give me good evidence that sin is a reality?

If you are a Christian, think about these questions: Does my Christian faith really affect my way of behaving—the way I decide what is right and wrong? How do I know this? What evidence can I point to? How did I decide between right and wrong today or this week? Did I base those decisions on my personal relationship to Christ? Does it bother me when proponents of the new morality call the Bible the words of men instead of the Word of God? Who's better off, the new moralists who claim that they can make decisions between right and wrong because they are "mature and responsible" or the Christian who practices Biblical morality and depends upon Christ to guide him and empower him? Is it a sign of weakness to depend on Christ? How do I depend on Christ?

TAKE ACTION . . .

Take a survey among friends and acquaintances and ask them this question: "Do you think Biblical morality is out of date?" In other words, do they think the Ten Commandments are relevant for the 20th century? If dialogue with friends or acquaintances from other races is available, ask them: "Does the Christian church practice the ethics it professes? What can Christians of all races do to improve the moral climate of America?"

Obtain and read Joseph Fletcher's book, *Situation Ethics*. Keep it as a cross reference text to study as you proceed through *It All Depends*.

CHAPTER 2
Those "sticky" situations

Just what is situation ethics? What kind of "situation" does it deal with?

Here are a few examples from Joseph Fletcher's book, *Situation Ethics*. Fletcher loves to prove his point by emphasizing the sticky problems in life—those dilemmas where it seems that you're wrong if you do and you're wrong if you don't. In addition, he not only finds sticky situations, but exceptional ones. For example, how would you handle this one? You are the father of a girl who is confined to a state mental hospital, a victim of radical schizophrenia. She has been raped by a fellow patient and has become pregnant. You are incensed and have demanded that an abortion be performed at once to end this unwanted pregnancy. The hospital refuses because criminal law forbids any abortion except a therapeutic one where the mother's life is at stake. In the hospital's eyes, any interference with an embryo is taking the life of an innocent being. Who is right? Who is wrong?*

Or perhaps you are an Arizona housewife and you want to terminate your pregnancy because you have been taking thalidomide, a drug that could cause your baby to be born hideously deformed. You cannot get an abortion in the United States, but you know that an abortion can be performed in Sweden and your husband is ready to fly you there. Should you go?**

Fletcher cites many other illustrations: the destroyer captain who has to decide between blowing up floating survivors of a sunken ship with depth bombs or letting the killer sub get away;*** the terminal cancer patient who can stop taking certain drugs and end his life immediately and thereby insure his wife of insurance money, or he can continue to take drugs and quite possibly prolong his life beyond the date of expiration of his insurance policy.****

These things "never happen to you," but . . .

The list of sticky situations goes on and on. An initial reaction by many people is: "These kind of things never happen to me." This may be very true, but Fletcher's question is: "What would you do if they did? And what would you do if similar things happen but not on such an extreme scale?"

*Situation Ethics, Joseph Fletcher. Copyright 1966, Westminster Press, p. 37–39.
**Situation Ethics, Fletcher, p. 135.
***Situation Ethics, Fletcher, p. 152.
****Situation Ethics, Fletcher, pp. 165, 166.

ALL OF US FACE STICKY SITUATIONS . . .

For example, what do you do when it is obvious that the diplomatic and even kindly thing to do is to "lie" rather than be rudely frank? All of us face sticky situations almost every day of our lives. As far as Mr. Fletcher is concerned, to try to apply a preset collection of rules or laws (such as the Ten Commandments) to situations demanding a decision between right and wrong is hopelessly "legalistic."

Fletcher claims that the writings of the Bible are useful to give information on ethical systems of the past, but these systems aren't necessarily binding for how man should act today. The Ten Commandments, for example, are useful as "guidelines" but they have no final authority in Fletcher's system.

In *Situation Ethics*, Fletcher stresses that there are only three basic approaches to making decisions between right and wrong: *legalistic*, *antinomian* (against all laws or principles), and *situational*.

I cannot tell a lie—your victim is hiding in the closet.

Do's and Don'ts for Christians

LEGALISM REDUCES CHRISTIANITY TO
DO'S AND DON'TS

Legalism, says Fletcher, is the approach to moral decision-making where "Solutions are preset and you can 'look them up' in a book—a Bible or a confessor's manual."*

Fletcher characterizes the legalistic approach to ethics with the following situation: An insane maniac approaches you waving a pistol, wanting to know the whereabouts of someone whom you have just seen enter a certain room. The maniac obviously wants to kill this person and so you are faced with a decision. Will you lie to the insane person and throw him off the trail of his intended victim or will you "tell him the truth" and let him find his victim and kill him?

According to Fletcher, "the legalist says that even if he tells the man escaped from the asylum where

Situation Ethics, Fletcher, p. 18.

ANTINOMIANISM: AGAINST ALL LAW

his intended victim is, if he finally murders him, at least only one sin has been committed (a murder), not two (lying as well)!"*

In Fletcher's opinion, the legalist puts the letter of the law ahead of love, mercy and justice. According to Fletcher, the legalist shouts, "Do the 'right' even if the sky falls down." Fletcher also quotes Mark Twain who describes the legalist as a "good man in the worst sense of the word."**

Antinomianism is the approach to decision-making situations in which a person uses no principles, rules, or maxims whatsoever. The word "antinomian" means literally "against the law." Martin Luther first used this term to describe Johannes Agricola and his views concerning the grace of God

*Situation Ethics, Joseph Fletcher, p. 26.
**Situation Ethics, Joseph Fletcher, p. 20.

and Christian freedom. Agricola taught that Christians were entirely free from the law—that is, the moral law laid down by Moses. Agricola argued that Christians were not required to keep the Ten Commandments. His reasoning was that justification by faith alone meant that absolutely no rules had to be kept, otherwise there would be the danger of a man being able to claim righteousness through his own good works.

In his *Situation Ethics,* Joseph Fletcher comments that the most subtle brand of lawlessness comes out of *existentialism,* a modern-day school of philosophy that stresses present experience.* For example, Jean Paul Sartre, a leading existentialist writer and philosopher, believes that there are no generally valid principles and there are no universal laws for human conduct.

Existentialists speak of the "incoherency of the world," and the "discontinuity between one experience and another." For the existentialist, every situation, every experience, is individual and particular. No experience has a connection to any other experience.

The existentialist is not concerned with the idea that what he might do today could affect many other people tomorrow and in the far distant future as well. The existentialist is not particularly concerned with the consequences of any given experience or act. He is more concerned with "now."

Although existentialist philosophers do not, as a rule, go around advocating revolution and violence, their viewpoint can quickly degenerate into just

Situation Ethics, Fletcher, p. 24.

that when practiced by hot heads and militants. The existentialist brand of antinomianism was present in varying degrees in many of the civil rights riots, student protests and the taking over of university facilities during the 1960's.

Becoming "fed up with the establishment" and reacting to rules and authority in a blind destructive rage is an illustration of how an existentialist feeling of meaninglessness and hopelessness can turn into lawlessness. When a person is in this state of mind, laws and rules mean nothing. What is important is to act, to demonstrate, to "do my own thing ... now!"

Situation ethics: a halfway house

For Joseph Fletcher, legalism and antinomianism are both undesirable and negative extremes to deciding between right and wrong. Fletcher's "halfway house" between these two extremes is his own system, "situation ethics." Fletcher believes that he escapes the web of legalism by setting aside all laws and rules and calling them merely "guidelines" and maxims that may or may not be useful. He believes he escapes the charge of antinomianism (lawlessness) by saying that he is at least willing to consult laws and use them as guides.

In addition, he maintains the one basic rule or principle that is valid for all ethical decision-making is the "law of love." By this, Fletcher means *agape* love—the kind of love that Jesus talked about in the summary commandment to love God and your neighbor. (See Matt. 22:34-40.) All other laws, rules, principles, ideals and norms are valid

I'm within the law, but I don't want any rules—none at all!

SITUATION ETHICS: SUGAR-COATED LAWLESSNESS

only if they happen to serve love in a given situation.

For Fletcher, all other rules and laws are only "rules of thumb" that can be tossed out, stretched, bent, or broken if necessary, in order to fill what he feels is the one basic unbreakable law—the law of love. Thus, for Fletcher, Exod. 20:14: "Thou shalt not commit adultery," is not binding, final or authoritative, but Rom. 13:8, "Owe no man any thing but to love one another," is.

Fletcher says that Christians have to grow up a little and quit trying to take their list of do's and don'ts along into the stream of life. Should you cheat on an exam if it means the difference between getting a scholarship and not having a chance for college? Would you drive a car without insurance "just once" if it meant doing a badly needed favor for a friend? To whom would you give the last pint of blood plasma? A drunken skid row bum, or the mother of three children?

According to Joseph Fletcher, the only law that matters is the law of love. In every given situation the individual must decide for himself just exactly how to serve the law of love according to his own opinion of the conditions and the consequences that are involved in that situation.

Situation ethics looks attractive, but . . .

At first glance, Joseph Fletcher's situation ethics seem to be practical and attractive. His "sticky cases" seem to make the Ten Commandments look almost obsolete. He seems to make sense as he points out the hopeless hypocrisy and inconsistency in trying to "live by the rule book."

Many a Christian would agree with Fletcher that he has seen all too many cases of legalistic nit-picking among those who profess to believe in Christ. If he is honest, the Christian will admit that he has been guilty of being legalistic more than once himself. Here, at last, seems to be the answer. Situation ethics appears to be the way to approach life realistically and live it as human beings actually experience it.

However, before embracing situation ethics as the way out of legalistic tribulation into the millennium of love and eternal bliss, the Christian should withhold judgment. Perhaps it would do the Christian well to know just exactly what Fletcher means when he talks about the "law of love."

And before stamping the Ten Commandments as "moral maxims that are useful guides but really

QUESTIONS FOR FLETCHER'S SITUATION ETHICS

obsolete as far as binding laws are concerned," the Christian should make sure that he's absolutely certain he has the resources, knowledge and ability to serve the "law of love" in every situation according to how he sees it.

Joseph Fletcher's sticky cases not only dramatize the dilemma faced by anyone who wants to live by the letter of the law; *these same cases also clearly point out that for any human being it is not always easy to do the "loving thing."* The question for the Christian is: "Does situation ethics really give me the direction I need to do the 'loving thing'?" Even more basic is the question, "Does situation ethics help me to do the will of God?"

Another thing the Christian should think about is whether Fletcher is right when he says that there are only three basic approaches to ethics: legalistic, lawless and situational. Could it be that there is a fourth alternative—an alternative that is found in the Bible itself? Every Christian owes it to himself, to society, and above all to God, to ask some hard questions of Joseph Fletcher and his system of situation ethics.

Are Biblical laws equal to legalism?

In *Situation Ethics*, Joseph Fletcher claims that Jesus stated His moral ethic in the "summary commandment" that He gave in Matt. 22:37-40. When the lawyer asked Christ what the great commandment of the law was, Christ told him, "Thou shalt love the Lord thy God with all thy heart, and with all thy soul, and with all thy mind. This is the first and great commandment. And the second is like unto it, Thou shalt love thy neighbour as thyself. On these two commandments hang all the law and the prophets."

The summary commandment is Fletcher's favorite "proof text" for reducing the Ten Commandments to only "rules of thumb" and making the only absolute in his system of situational ethics the "law of love." The question is, however, is this the complete picture of what Christ taught or of what the Bible teaches?

Christ also plainly stated that he had not come to do away with the law but to fulfill the law. (See

Matt. 5:17.) He went right on to say that until heaven and earth passed away, not one dot or comma would pass from the law until all of the law had been fulfilled. (See Matt. 5:18.) And then Jesus capped His statement by saying that whoever would break the least of the commandments and teach others to break them would be called the least in the Kingdom of Heaven. But whoever would do the commandments and teach them would be called great in the Kingdom of Heaven. (See Matt. 5:19.)

Of course, Fletcher has an answer for this. On page 70 of *Situation Ethics*, he writes:

"Often we hear quoted the Judaizing phrase in Matt. 5:17-20 (and Luke 16:17), 'Not an iota, not a dot, will pass from the law,' and 'Whoever relaxes one of the least of these commandments' shall be small potatoes in the Kingdom. Literalizers or fundamentalists take these phrases, however inconsistent they are with the rest of the Gospels and Paul's letters, as a law requiring law! ... The love commandment (the Shema of Deut. 6:4,5 combined with Lev. 19:18, in Mark 12:29-32, etc.) is, so runs the argument, Jesus' summary of the *law!*"[*]

By "literalizers and fundamentalists" Fletcher refers to people who believe that the Bible is the inspired Word of God, people who take the Bible as authoritative truth. All of these "literalizers" are wrong, according to Fletcher, because they would believe that Jesus really meant what He said in Matt. 5:17-20. Yet, nowhere in *Situation Ethics* does Fletcher explain what he says on page 70 of his book. He never does explain what he means by

Situation Ethics, Joseph Fletcher, p. 70.

27

I try to live by the Ten Commandments.

Sorry to hear that you're a legalist.

SITUATION ETHICS DISTORTS BIBLICAL MORALITY

saying that Jesus' words in Matthew 5 are "inconsistent with the rest of the Gospels and Paul's letters. In short, Fletcher does not answer the question at all. He resorts to the favorite argument of the liberal or neo-orthodox theologian who says that a certain part of the Bible doesn't really apply because it doesn't have as much authority as the parts he wants to quote.

In short, Fletcher unfairly confuses Biblical law (the Ten Commandments) with "legalism" *which is an attitude of using the law in the wrong way.*

Furthermore, since Jesus condemned the legalism of the Pharisees by word and deed, it is a fair question to ask if He entered situations with no real rules but only "moral maxims" and "rules of thumb" from the Pentateuch (the first five books of the Bible). On the contrary, while condemning legalism, Jesus lived by the law.

On the Mount of Temptation (Matt. 4:1-11) Jesus banished Satan not by asking: "How can I show love to the most people in this situation?" but by quoting Scripture. Jesus had the basic decisions of life to make when Satan asked Jesus to bow down and worship him with the whole world as the prize. Jesus did not "ponder the situation" by thinking through how He could best distribute the greatest good to the greatest number of people if the whole world were His.

When Satan asked Jesus to throw Himself down from the temple to show that God would not let Him be hurt, Jesus did not ponder the inestimable amount of good that this act might bring to a great number of people who would see the power of God in action and believe in Him.

When tempted, Jesus "lived by the law"

And when Jesus refused Satan's temptation to turn stones into bread by telling him that man does not live by bread alone, there was no reason to think that He was telling Satan that love was the only real standard for life. The point here is that Jesus operated according to "rules that God had already laid down." Every one of Jesus' replies to Satan was from the Old Testament—from the "law" itself. In resisting temptation, Jesus "lived by the law."

But there is a difference between living by the law and living legalistically. Joseph Fletcher sets up a "straw man" called legalism and easily demolishes it and so he should. But Joseph Fletcher makes a serious mistake when he equates that same "straw man" with Biblical morality (what the Bible really teaches about right and wrong). Biblical laws are not made of straw. Biblical laws are strands of steel which God uses to bring men to Himself. As Paul wrote in Rom. 7:7:

"Well then, am I suggesting that these laws of God are evil? Of course not! No, the law is not sinful but it was the law that showed me my sin. I would never have known the sin in my heart—the evil desires that are hidden there—if the law had not said, 'You must not have evil desires in your heart.'" *(Living New Testament)*.

The Law reveals your need of Christ

In short, men make "rules of thumb," God makes authoritative laws. In passing, it is also interesting to recall Fletcher's comment that the "Judaizing" phrase in Matt. 5:19, about forbidding anyone to teach others to break the law, is supposedly in contradiction to other writings by Paul. It would seem, however, that Rom. 7:7 doesn't contradict Matt. 5:19 at all. Christ not only came to fulfill the law, He came to redeem men from their sins. And Christ knew what the law could do: show men their sin and help them recognize their need of Him.

And here is a key point: the law is useful. The law is authoritative, *but you also need Christ.* Without Him, your attempts to "obey the law" soon turn into legalism.

One of the most perceptive critics of situation ethics is William Banowsky, Ph.D., vice-president of Pepperdine College in Los Angeles and minister in the Church of Christ. Banowsky points out that situation ethics is correct in condemning the hopeless swamp of hypocrisy and contradictions in legalism. Banowsky comments:

"Hence, a businessman abuses his employees and has a reputation for sharp if not shady dealing, but feels pious in Sunday school because he neither drinks nor smokes. Another man considers himself moral because he avoids 'cuss words,' but thinks nothing of referring to a fellow human being as a 'nigger.' Or a girl is willing to park with any boy she dates and embraces every form of sexual stimulation yet thinks herself chaste, so long as she stops short of the magic line which keeps the fragile gem of virginity technically intact. Christ's cutting remark about straining out the gnat and swallowing the camel fits such moral manipulation, as does his criticism of paying tithes of mint, anise and cummin while ignoring the weightier matters of justice, mercy and faith. 'These ought ye to have done and not to leave the other undone' (Matt. 23:23,24)."*

Banowsky also observes that you are seeking a cheap way out if you try to reduce choices between right and wrong to a "tidy list." "Righteousness," says Banowsky, "cannot be cut down to manageable size by mimeographing a sheet of do's and don'ts."**

According to Banowsky, Christ's approach to right and wrong faces the realities of life and the fact that all moral judgments are not clear black and white choices. But because life is not an open-shut case of black and white choices doesn't mean that you need to join Joseph Fletcher in saying ". . . there are no rules, none at all."**

The answer to legalism is not tossing out all the rules, except the "law of love." The answer to legalism is not deciding, as Joseph Fletcher says, "If

---

*See "The New Morality: The Christian Solution," two sermons by Dr. William Banowsky published in booklet form by R. B. Sweet Co., Inc., Box 4055, Austin, Texas, Copyright 1968, Campus Evangelism.
**Situation Ethics, Fletcher, p. 55.

It's not wrong to commit adultery or fornication unless someone gets hurt.

FLETCHER MIGHT AS WELL SAY IT'S NOT WRONG TO WALK AGAINST THE RED LIGHT UNLESS SOMEONE GETS HURT

people do not believe that it is wrong to have sexual relations outside of marriage, it isn't; unless they hurt themselves, their partners, or others."[*] In this way Fletcher neatly crosses out the basic rule, "You should not commit fornication or adultery." He replaces it with his own absolute law— the law of love. And therefore, he reasons that it is not wrong to have sexual relations outside of marriage *unless* someone gets hurt. This is like saying that it is not wrong to walk across the street during rush hour against the red light *unless* someone gets hurt. Or, it is not wrong to drive 90 miles per hour in a 15 miles per hour school zone *unless* someone gets hurt.[**]

---

[*]*Situation Ethics*, Fletcher, p. 77.
[**]Fletcher might disagree with these analogies by pointing out that walking against the light or driving 90 miles an hour in a 15 miles per hour zone would not be "acting responsibly in love." But it can also be argued that having sexual relations with someone outside of the basic personal commitment made in marriage vows is also no way to "act responsibly in love" and much more will be said about this in the discussion of the *Playboy Philosophy* in chapters 6, 7, and 8.

About the only thing that is clear at this point of Fletcher's thinking is that he is unclear. He seems to contradict himself. He seems to want to keep his ice cream in the freezer and still have it for supper. He assures everyone that he is not lawless, yet he wants to work under no binding rules. He wants to use his own subjective opinions for deciding what is right and wrong. The one binding rule he will follow is the "law of love," but even this is open to his personal opinions and interpretations "according to the situation."

Opinions differ on what is "loving"

It is not too hard to see that in the practice of situation ethics, one person's opinion will be precisely the opposite of another. Where, then, is the "right"? How can the person who practices situation ethics know when he is really doing the "loving thing"?

The issue boils down to this: can you replace all absolute rules, such as those in the Ten Commandments, with one big absolute rule and call it the law of love? Or do men need these absolutes like the Ten Commandments in order to really obey the law of love in the first place? If men don't need these other rules, if they are capable of obeying the law of love according to their own judgment and their own "loving natures," then Fletcher is right and situation ethics is a sound system.

But if men are not able to obey this law of love out of their own loving natures and if they are not capable of always determining just what the loving thing in a situation is, then they do need these other

ONE MAN'S LOVE IS ANOTHER MAN'S LUMPS

absolutes, even though there are still situations where "exceptions" occur.*

But because he can think of "sticky situations," exceptional cases where it appears that you must violate one law in order to obey another, Joseph Fletcher feels that the only thing to do is be ready to set aside all the rules, use your own loving judgment and "do the loving thing."

Joseph Fletcher is so confident about man's ability to do the loving thing that another question about his system arises: Does he really understand the nature of sin? The answer to this one is in the next chapter.

TAKE TIME...

Use the following ideas to take time to apply the Bible to your life and any situations you face.

A replacement for the Ten Commandments?

In answer to the lawyer's question: "Sir, which is the most important command in the laws of Moses?" Jesus

*The Christian's answer to those "exceptional cases" is trust in God's grace and forgiveness, not his own rationalizing that what he is doing is something "good and right." See Chapter 5.

34

summed up the law this way: [37]" 'Love the Lord your God with all your heart, soul, and mind.' [38,39]This is the first and greatest commandment. The second most important is similar: 'Love your neighbor as much as you love yourself.' [40]All the other commandments and all the demands of the prophets stem from these two laws and are fulfilled if you obey them. Keep only these and you will find that you are obeying all the others" (Matt. 22:37-40, *Living New Testament*).

How do these verses read to you? Do they give you the idea that the Ten Commandments are no longer binding and authoritative and that all you have to do is obey the "law of love"? Why? Why not? Do you believe that you can fulfill the law by getting rid of part of it? Why? Why not? Also, why does Jesus point out that in keeping the first and second commandments to love God and your neighbor that you will then be obeying all the other commandments? If those other laws are not authoritative, what difference does it make if you fail to obey the "two great commandments"?

The laws stay on the books.

Although Joseph Fletcher likes to quote Jesus' summary commandment in Matt. 22:37-40 to prove his case for situation ethics, he has little answer for another remark by Christ:

[17]"Don't misunderstand why I have come—it isn't to cancel the laws of Moses and the warnings of the prophets. No, I came to fulfill them, and to make them all come true. [18]With all the earnestness I have I say: Every law in the Book will continue until its purpose is achieved. [19]And so if anyone breaks the least commandment, and teaches others to, he shall be the least in the Kingdom of Heaven. But those who teach God's laws *and obey them* shall be great in the Kingdom of Heaven" (Matt. 5:17-19, *Living New Testament*).

Look up the word "fulfill" in the dictionary. What does it mean? Joseph Fletcher is strangely silent in *Situation Ethics* on the meaning of this word "fulfill." Why is he so silent?

TAKE INVENTORY . . .

Go back and look again at the "sticky situations" cited from Joseph Fletcher's book *Situation Ethics* at the beginning of this chapter. According to Fletcher's premise, there are only three possible approaches to any moral decision: legalistic, lawless, or his approach—situational. What would your approach be to these sticky problems, which seem to argue effectively for Fletcher's point of view?

For example, pages 37-39 of *Situation Ethics*, Fletcher describes the case of the rape of the mental patient who subsequently became pregnant. According to Fletcher, the situationist would say the father was right in requesting an abortion, and only a legalist would refuse an abortion in this case. In bringing up abortion as an example of a "sticky moral situation" Fletcher chooses a most controversial area.* What Fletcher is trying to do, of course, is to put the reader in a legalistic corner because he believes in the commandment of "Thou shalt not kill." Fletcher could just as easily do this with a situation regarding taking the enemy's life in war or in taking the life of an intruder who had broken into your home with the intent of killing you. The sixth commandment does not deal with prevention of justifiable homicide, but with murder. There are many reputable Christians who feel that in certain extreme cases, abortion is justifiable or necessary. But, in stating their beliefs, they do not deny the validity of the commandment "Thou shalt not kill." Careful analysis of

---

*For discussion of abortion, see Chapter 8.

many of Joseph Fletcher's sticky cases shows that they are not as "sticky" as they are "tricky."

TAKE ACTION . . .

Observe your own behavior, the behavior of your parents and of others around you in the coming weeks to see if you can find examples of practicing "situation ethics." See if you can analyze why people make certain decisions. Are they trying to solve the immediate needs and problems of the moment or are they looking ahead to long-range consequences for what they do?

Also look through the daily newspaper for examples of moral choices that people have made where there has not been a clear-cut choice between right and wrong. For example, find stories on disputes between labor and management and analyze the ethical questions involved. Are the workers asking for more than is rightfully theirs? Is management being fair and living up to its agreements?

Another area is disagreements between nations. Are treaties being broken? Are promises not being kept? Is it obvious that one nation is simply trying to exploit the other?

Stories on legal problems and scandal are loaded with moral implications. Analyze how politicians handle tax money, why they vote for certain laws and why they refuse to OK others. Try to find examples of politicians who are not afraid to stand for their principles instead of drifting with the tide of political expediency.

Analyze your own attitude toward decisions on right and wrong. Are you more of a legalist than you thought you were? Perhaps you are more of a situationist than you thought you were. See if you can determine not how legal or how situational you are, but how Biblical you are in making your decisions and what part your commitment to Christ plays in these decisions.

CHAPTER 3

Weak link
in the
chain?

In the foreword to *Situation Ethics*, Joseph Fletcher illustrates his basic ideas about moral choices by telling how a friend of his arrived in St. Louis at the end of a political campaign. As they rode along in a cab, the cab driver explained that his family had been Republican for many years and that he himself was a Republican. Fletcher's friend then told the cabby that he assumed that he would be voting for "Senator so-and-so," but the cabby replied: "No, there are times when a man has to push his principles aside and do the right thing." According to Fletcher, that St. Louis cabby is "the hero" of *Situation Ethics*.*

With a St. Louis cab driver of unknown spiritual condition set up as the hero of his book on Christian ethics, Fletcher then moves on to nominate a "co-hero"— the "Rainmaker" from the play of the

---

Situation Ethics, Joseph Fletcher. Copyright 1966, Westminster Press, p. 13.

same name by M. Richard Nash. (The stage play was also made into a film starring Burt Lancaster.)

The plot of the "Rainmaker" revolves around a visit made to a ranch by the Rainmaker, a man who made his living by convincing ranchers that he could bring rain for their parched crops and herds. While staying at the ranch, the Rainmaker meets the rancher's daughter, a lonely spinster type. Rainmaker "feels sorry" for this poor girl and takes her out to the hayloft where they make quite a bit more than small talk at midnight.

According to Joseph Fletcher, the Rainmaker's intention is to restore this girl's sense of womanliness and give her hope for marriage and children. The next morning, the girl's elder brother learns what happened and grabs a pistol, threatening to shoot the Rainmaker for his crime. But her father, who Fletcher calls a "wise old rancher," grabs the pistol away from the brother, saying, "Noah, you're so full of what's right you can't see what's good."*

Is the "wise old rancher" really wise and right? Is Noah really so full of what's right that he can't see what's good? There will be more said about this later, but something to recognize in these "co-heroes" of situation ethics is that their "situations" are typical of "real life." Doesn't the wise old

*Fletcher cites p. 99 in the book *The Rainmaker* by M. Richard Nash, Bantam Books, Inc. Copyright 1957. He also calls attention to Robert Anderson's *Tea and Sympathy* (The New American Library of World Literature, Inc., 1956, especially Act 3). The plot of *Tea and Sympathy* revolves around how an older woman "benevolently" commits adultery with a young man to prove to him that he is not a homosexual. Fletcher also refers to an English movie called *The Mark* in which a man is sexually attracted to little girls until a woman his own age seduces him and releases him from his pathological tendencies. These are some of the "case studies" that situationists like to use to prove that in some cases "adultery and fornication is a good and right thing."

THE MESSAGE IN "THE RAINMAKER" IS THAT FORNICATION CAN BE GOOD AND THAT MAKES IT RIGHT.

rancher sound like a real flesh and blood kind of guy? Doesn't the cabby sound like he's for real? Like he's honest and forthright? No paragons of legalistic piety are these co-heroes. They are real life types—the kind you meet in this everyday world.

And that is just the point: early in his book, Fletcher makes it clear that his situation ethics are *Christian* ethics. And yet, throughout his book, again and again, he cites secular situations. The point is not that Christian ethics can't be used in secular situations; the point is: the people in these sticky situations that Fletcher uses are never identified as Christians, Communists, or agnostics. They are just "plain folks," the kind of people you would find in any secular society.

Joseph Fletcher's use of "secular situations" to illustrate Christian ethics is extremely significant. As defined in Chapter 1, "secular" means to be concerned about the values of this world, the immediate needs in the situation, the practical solution to a given problem. To hear the advocates of the new morality tell it, the church has got to face facts today: it lives in a secular world and it must adjust to the times and the situation. This is essentially the theme of Harvey Cox in *The Secular City*.

Canon Douglas Rhymes, one of the leading advocates of situation ethics in England, echoes Cox's concern with understanding the nature of secular man. "There will be the need to find a common moral ground between the believer and the nonbeliever, between the Christian and the humanist," writes Rhymes as he suggests beginning a dialogue with nonbelievers to discover ways to reconcile Christianity and secular views.*

All of this sounds very sensible. After all, the Christian church has been misunderstood too many times in the past. Shouldn't it learn how to live in a secular society, how to live on "common moral ground" with secular and humanistic thinkers?

That all depends. It all depends on what you think the purpose of the Christian church is. Christ made it plain that He had not come to "get along with secular society" but that He had come to save men from their sins, *to change secular society and give secularists a hope they didn't have*. The Biblical record makes it plain that every time believers in God have compromised with secular society in an attempt to find a "common ground" they have not gained ground but lost it.

For example, the main problem in Corinth

*"The New Morality, What, Why, and Why Not?" Douglas A. Rhymes, *Religion and Life*, Spring 1966, pp. 173, 174.

41

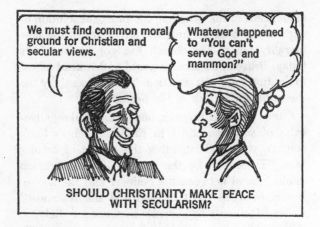

SHOULD CHRISTIANITY MAKE PEACE
WITH SECULARISM?

among the Corinthian Christians was not really immorality, dissension or even bad table manners at communion. The main problem was the secular spirit that had crept into the church. The Corinthian Christians had returned to following the basic prevailing philosophy of the secular world—nothing mattered beyond what satisfied immediate desire.

Before getting too chummy with the secular world, the Christian should remember that he may be in the secular world but the Bible plainly states that he should not be "of it." (See John 17:15-21; I Cor. 5:7-10.) In his book *Not Like Ordinary Men*, Laurence Kinney points out that secular man basically assumes that the only kind of knowledge he needs is of "things"—the tangible, the material. Many people today actually subscribe to the view that the only kind of knowledge that you can have for sure is what you can experience with your senses. There are two schools of thought that dominate the thinking of secular men today, and both of them stress the supremacy of knowledge through the senses.

Humanism believes in man's perfectability

One of these schools is *humanism.* The humanist basically believes in man's essential goodness and perfectability. Give man the right living conditions, enough education, enough job opportunities and he will reach to the heights. The whole emphasis of humanism is on "what man can do, what man can see, what man can feel, what man can experience."

As for moral choices, the humanist has no hang-up, no "book of rules" called the Bible. Indeed, the humanist denies the existence of God and the necessity of any kind of God-given system of morals. Morality is a matter of "personal opinion." Let your conscience be your guide. Observe the evidence and the "situation." Then decide according to your own moral code.

Working hand in hand with humanism is the view called *naturalism.* For the naturalist, nature is God and the scientist is the high priest. Man will discover all through science—even the mystery of life itself. For the naturalist, man is a highly complex animal who has evolved from lower forms of life. Human beings act on instinct like any other animal. Everyone is a tool of everyone else and all of us are captives of our drives and reflexes.*

Why all this talk about secularism and its two step-children—humanism and naturalism? Why all the emphasis that the secularist is basically con-

---

*Information on humanism and naturalism based on "Morality on the College Campus," Charles Lantay, *Church Herald,* October 23, 1964, p. 20.

HUMANISTS AND NATURALISTS ARE BOSOM BUDDIES

cerned with satisfying the needs and desires such as food, drink, sex, security, etc.?

Do not misunderstand. There is nothing basically wrong with being hungry or thirsty. There is nothing wrong with the human sex drive and there is nothing wrong with the human need for security, self-esteem, love, etc. But what can and does often go wrong is that human beings (including Christians) start putting these needs and desires ahead of God.

When you put your needs and desires ahead of God you commit sin—rebellion against God in an active or a passive way. Today, the secular minded man rebels against God more passively than actively. In other words, the secularist doesn't go around shaking his fist at God and deliberately shouting blasphemies toward the heavens. Rather, he simply doesn't give God much thought. He has no time for God; God just doesn't fit into his plans.

However, Fletcher's propensity to use secular situations to illustrate his system of "Christian eth-

ics" plus Fletcher's amazing, even naive trust in the
ability of secular man to "do the loving thing"
brings up another question about his system:

Situation ethics: A "secular view" of sin?

For a secularist, sin is a very relative term. Mention the word sin in secular company (in the office,
at school, etc.) and you get back the idea that a
"sinner" is a cross between Adolph Hitler, public
enemy number one and Sirhan Sirhan.

Or, people often go on the defensive, especially if
they think they are talking to "one of those Bible-
banging Christians." They start to justify their use
of tobacco and alcohol. They point out that they're
not as bad as a lot of people they know, etc., etc.
They see themselves as quite capable of doing the
right thing more often than the wrong thing. They
consider themselves to have their share of "Christian love" for the world and mankind.

All this, of course, fits in nicely with Joseph
Fletcher's approach to situation ethics. Fletcher's
approach is appealing because it puts a strong emphasis on love, which is positive, and he criticizes
legalism, which is negative. In short, Joseph
Fletcher tells the St. Louis cab driver, the Rainmaker, and everyone else to never mind about all
those hairy rules . . . just go out there and love
everybody! All of us are to put on "Love and do as
you please" buttons and sally forth into the world
equipped with the most advanced ethical system
yet to be devised by man. With the law of love as
our supreme authority and the Ten Commandments
tucked in nicely with our copies of *How to Win*

SITUATION ETHICS TRUSTS
SINFUL MAN TO ACT UNSELFISHLY

Friends and Influence People and other "guide-lines," we will face each situation and make the loving choice.

Just a situational minute...

Isn't there something in the Bible about man being a sinner? Isn't it true that all of us are quite capable of making mistakes, and isn't it also true that while we might see one solution as the loving thing in a certain situation, someone else might see it just exactly the other way? Perhaps situation ethics makes the road a little more slippery than we first thought.

A basic criticism of situation ethics is that it can easily be distorted and actually become far more dangerous and destructive than outright lawlessness.

Kyle Haselden, outspoken critic of the new morality, observes that if right and wrong are relative terms, then everything is up to personal and subjective opinion. What is right and loving for one person might be evil and wrong for another.*

*Morality and the Mass Media, Kyle Haselden. Copyright 1968. Broadman Press, Chapter 1.

46

We all have our "hidden agenda"

The hard fact of life is that while people might say that they want to do the right thing, more often than not they have a "hidden agenda." They are more interested in pleasing themselves than God. They are more interested in loving themselves than in loving God or others, and no amount of urging by Joseph Fletcher to get out there and love responsibly changes the way things really are.

Man's basic moral problem is sin—and this doesn't mean that sin is limited to killers and tyrants or that it is to be confused with violation of certain cultural taboos. Sin is rebellion against God in active or passive form. Sin is saying, "Flake off, God. I'm busy."

The Bible recognizes the basic flaw in man—sin (which is the weak link in situation ethics). Scripture records this accurate (but not too positive) thought: "The heart is deceitful above all things, and desperately wicked: who can know it?" (Jer. 17:9). Paul, the apostle, had a lot to say about sin and he didn't leave anyone out: the pagans, the "good citizens" and even the religious church-goers all came under condemnation from God. "All have sinned, and come short of the glory (the high standard) of God" (Rom. 3:23).

Is the Bible realistic or just plain negative? There is a difference between the two. Your answer depends on how you want to interpret the facts. Too many people in this world just aren't able (or just don't care) to work and strive to be moral. Joseph Fletcher's system of situation ethics would be most attractive if people possessed the basic resources

47

and ability to be ideally moral and good, but people aren't ideally moral and good. The world is not ideal because sin is in the world and sin is in people.

Because of sin, laws are necessary. Because of sin, laws are not "negative," they are realistic. Laws recognize man's need for guidance and direction, and this means more than being told to "do the loving thing in every situation." The point is that without laws, doing the "loving thing" is meaningless. Without laws, you cannot possibly determine what the loving, fair or just thing is.

New morality critic Vernon Grounds reduces the matter to a basic choice. You can follow the Ten Commandments or you can take Joseph Fletcher's road labeled the law of love. Granted, following the Ten Commandments is no guarantee that you would do the right thing every time. You could, in fact, do the wrong thing every time, if you applied the Ten Commandments legalistically. But the Ten Commandments are not legalism. Legalism is an attitude that uses the Ten Commandments in the wrong way. If, however, you use the Ten Commandments in an unselfish, unflinching, open and honest way, as you seek the mind of Christ and the will of God, you will do the right thing much more often than if you merely used the commandments as "rules of thumb" and put your personal opinions in charge.*

*See "The New Morality: What's Wrong with the New View of Right?" Vernon Grounds. *His* magazine, October, 1967. Dr. Grounds is a holder of a Ph.D. degree from Drew University. He is president of Conservative Baptist Theological Seminary in Denver, Colo. and also teaches apologetics and philosophy there. In 1967-68 he published a series of articles in *His* analyzing the claims of the new morality and situation ethics.

A WARPED OVEREMPHASIS ON "CRUCIFYING THE FLESH" IS NOT THE GOOD NEWS OF THE GOSPEL

Joseph Fletcher calls his situation ethics "Christian" which by definition means "sacred and devoted to God; of Christ." Actually, his system is a wide-open invitation to secularism—putting the need of the moment and personal desires ahead of anything else. If obeying the law of *agape* love is a matter of personal opinion, then who is to say what is right or wrong? The new morality actually puts man in the driver's seat. Man "calls the shots" the way he wants to.

Situation ethics not only has a secular view of sin; it has a naive view of sin. The Bible, on the other hand, takes a realistic view of man's weakness and needs. Talking about sin is not popular. It is much more "positive" to talk about man's potential —his desire to do the loving thing, etc.

It must be granted, too, that there has been too much preaching in the name of Christ that has dwelt on sin so long and so hard that the way some people seem to tell it, Christianity is nothing but negative, depressing, degrading and disgusting. A warped overemphasis on sin and "crucifying the flesh" is not the real message of the Bible any more than the Ten Commandments are legalism.

The real message of the Bible is that man is a sinner, but God loves him anyway, and has done something to get him out of a hopeless predicament. God not only offers secular man salvation, He offers His own wisdom and guidance for making moral choices.

Meanwhile, back in the hayloft

And that brings us back to the Rainmaker—that noble hero of the hayloft who intended to restore a sense of womanliness to the rancher's daughter and give her hope of marriage and children by fornicating with her. Remember that Fletcher calls the Rainmaker "co-hero" of his book *Situation Ethics*. Apparently, in Fletcher's opinion, the action taken by Rainmaker is illustrative of how a person would act "responsibly in love" as he applied situation ethics in his moral decision-making.

Fletcher doesn't tell us if the Rainmaker is a Christian, a Moslem, a Hindu or a Hottentot. But he does make it plain that he believes that the Rainmaker is an example of how to practice Christian ethics. So, let us examine the Rainmaker's noble example.

The facts are these: he has engaged in sexual intercourse with a woman out of wedlock, a practice commonly referred to as fornication. (Of course, if the Rainmaker has a wife somewhere back east, that makes it adultery, but since we don't really know that, let's go on.) Suppose he had done this with the girl's open and even enthusiastic consent. Does this make his action "right"?

Apparently one thing makes the Rainmaker right: *his good intentions.* But do good intentions grant you some kind of infallible power to rise above the limitations of sin and the other weaknesses that are part of being a human being? Do good intentions give you some mysterious power to look into the future to be sure that what you do will "turn out for the best"? There is an old cliché, "The road to hell is paved with good intentions." It might be added that so is the road to prison, mental institutions and homes for unwed mothers.

God's in His heaven, all's right on the ranch

Let's go back to the wise old rancher for a moment—the girl's father, who apparently approved of Rainmaker's action (perhaps he had been a "rainmaker" at one time or another himself). Wise old father rancher tells Noah, the irate elder son, that he is so full of what's right he doesn't know what's good.

Is the rancher speaking secularly or from God's point of view? Situation ethics is supposedly Christian ethics. Therefore, it would seem to follow that in this situation God is in His heaven and all is right on the ranch. At least God is smiling on the Rainmaker and the rancher while frowning on the "legalistic" brother.

Granted, Noah's intention to shoot the Rainmaker could hardly be called a loving intention. Noah shows no signs of the key Christian virtue called forgiveness. For Fletcher's purposes, Noah plays the part of the legalist, concerned only with the law and his sister's honor (meaning his own reputation and that of his entire family).

Notice the way Fletcher brings in his three-fold approach to Christian ethics here: there is the legalistic approach (Noah's); there is lawlessness (against which Noah is protesting); and there is "situationism"—Rainmaker's noble act to restore this girl's sense of womanhood. Biblical ethics never really gets into the act, but we are assured that this scene is an example of Christian love and doing the right thing.

Of course, the girl—whom Rainmaker obviously does not intend to marry—is left facing some interesting possibilities: the discomforts and risks of pregnancy without the care and sympathy of a husband, the shame and stigma of rearing a child who will keep wondering where his daddy is.

Should Rainmaker get the benefit or the doubt?

There is also the very real possibility that exactly what Rainmaker hoped to achieve—a better psychological state for the girl in which she would enjoy a renewed sense of womanliness and hopes of marriage and children—would be exactly what he would fail to provide. Women are funny about things like going to bed or to haylofts with a man. Even though they know that the man is using them, they still try to kid themselves into believing that "maybe he does really care for me after all. Maybe he will stay and marry me." There is the very real possibility that Rainmaker could have ridden into the sunset leaving an even more dejected, depressed and introverted girl behind him than the one he met when he rode in.

The point is, all men are fallible sinners, and they need more to guide their moral choices than "good intentions" to fulfill the law of love in the situation. As for the Rainmaker being co-hero of *Situation Ethics,* and therefore an example of how to practice Christian ethics, one is left feeling just a bit skeptical. Of course it may be that such skepticism is legalistic and unwarranted.

Undoubtedly Rainmaker had a long season of prayer before he took the girl to the hayloft. He probably sweat great drops in anguish and concern as he prayed, "Lord, this girl needs a sense of womanliness and it looks like I am the one to give it to her. Lord, I will fornicate with this girl and thereby do Your will. In Jesus' name. Amen."

(Ahem.) It is hard to understand how Joseph Fletcher—obviously a man of great learning—could offer Rainmaker as co-hero of his book and therefore by logical deduction, a key example of how to practice situation ("Christian") ethics. Fletcher seems to be on much better ground when he talks about maniacs looking for their victims and would you lie to them or not? He even makes a better case for having an abortion if the baby's father is a rapist.

With Rainmaker, Joseph Fletcher reveals clearly the mortally weak link in his entire system of ethics. Fletcher trusts sinful, limited man to do the loving thing according to the situation, with no binding rules upon him except a law of love that he can interpret as he sees fit. Fletcher seeks to escape the frying pan of legalism (and don't we all?) but jumping into the fire is hardly the way to go about it.

TAKE TIME . . .

Use the following ideas to take time to apply the Bible to your life and any situation you face.

Secular city revisited.

[10]"As the Scriptures say, 'No one is good—no one in all the world is innocent.' [11]No one has ever really followed God's paths, or even truly wanted to. [12]Every one has turned away; all have gone wrong. No one anywhere has kept on doing what is right; not one. [13]Their talk is foul and filthy like the stench from an open grave. Their tongues are loaded with lies. Everything they say has in it the sting and poison of deadly snakes. [14]Their mouths are full of cursing and bitterness. [15]They are quick to kill, hating anyone who disagrees with them. [16]Wherever they go they leave misery and trouble behind them. [17]And they have never known what it is to feel secure or enjoy God's blessing. [18]They care nothing about God nor what He thinks of them" (Rom. 3:10-18, *Living New Testament*).

This is Paul's summation of the record of mankind in God's sight. Do you think he is too negative? Is he accurate? Which of the facts in these verses is most descriptive of the secular point of view? See especially v. 18.

The Bible has a great deal more to say about sin. But while Scripture condemns man, it also offers man the good news that God has done something about sin. For a Biblical view of the universality of sin see I Kings 8:46; Ps. 53:3; Prov. 20:9; Isa. 53:6; 64:6; Rom. 3:23; I John 1:8. The Bible speaks about how sin can deceive man: Rom. 7:11; I Tim. 2:14; II Tim. 3:13; Titus 3:3; Heb. 3:13. For verses on what God has done about sin see Heb. 2:9; 9:28; I Peter 2:24; 3:18; I John 3:5,16.

54

Jesus and the adulterous woman: a situation.

In John 8:1-11 is the account of how the Pharisees brought a woman in adultery to Jesus and demanded that He pronounce the death penalty on her. Because Jesus knew they were trying to trap Him into saying something they could use against Him, He stooped down and wrote in the dust with His finger: "'They kept demanding an answer, so He stood up again and said, 'All right, hurl the stones at her until she dies. But only he who never sinned may throw the first!' ⁸Then He stooped down again and wrote some more in the dust. ⁹And the Jewish leaders slipped away one by one, beginning with the eldest, until only Jesus was left in front of the crowd with the woman. ¹⁰Then Jesus stood up again and said to her, 'Where are your accusers? Didn't even one of them condemn you?'

¹¹'No, sir,' she said.

And Jesus said, 'Neither do I. Go and sin no more'" (John 8:7-11, *Living New Testament*).

Do you think Jesus applied situation ethics to this woman's plight? After all He refused to condemn her to death as demanded by the law of Moses. But if He wanted to be a real situationist He would have called her active adultery a good and right thing, would He not? What did He call it? A crucial point to remember in analyzing Joseph Fletcher's situation ethics is to remember that the Bible is neither all love nor all law but that it is a balance of the two. It is like two sides of a coin. What Joseph Fletcher is trying to get you to do is to play his kind of game which has the rule: "heads (love) I win, tails (law) you lose."

TAKE INVENTORY . . .

Go back to the opening of this chapter and the remark of the St. Louis cabby (co-hero of *Situation*

Ethics) who was willing to put aside his principles and do the right thing. Analyze the cabby's statement. Granted, he was talking about politics and what he probably was really trying to say was that he was willing to put aside his Republican views and prejudices and vote for a man from another party whom he believed could better serve the people. But Fletcher tries to actually put words in the cabby's mouth. Do you think that a person can really do the right thing by laying aside all his principles?

What about your own attitude toward making moral choices? Do you believe you could successfully use Joseph Fletcher's system in a world where people often see right and wrong very differently? On the other hand, the Bible does not offer you a "mimeographed list of do's and don'ts" for every moral choice you have to make. As Joseph Fletcher points out, the Ten Commandments can easily be turned into legalism. How do you prevent that from happening?

TAKE ACTION . . .

Take an opinion poll on the question: "Do you really believe man is born in sin or does he become a sinner because of his environment?" Also ask this question: "What is sin?" Categorize the answers as Christian or secular.

As you face moral decisions, try analyzing not only what seems to be the "practical solution for the immediate problem" but also the long-range consequences of what you will do. Does it seem that the long-range consequences often cancel out what seems to be a very "practical solution" at the moment?

CHAPTER 4

Situation ethics:
Christian or ???

In 1841 the passenger ship *William Brown* struck an iceberg off Newfoundland and two boats got away with survivors. One carried the captain and a few passengers and was picked up shortly. The other boat contained the first mate, seven seamen and 32 passengers, just about twice its capacity.

Because of the rough seas, the overloaded craft threatened to sink at any moment, and the mate ordered most of the men in the boat into the sea. The men refused to go and a seaman named Holmes threw them in. Later when the remaining survivors were rescued, Holmes was tried for murder and convicted with a "recommendation of mercy."*

This is one of the "sticky situations" that Joseph Fletcher points to as an example of *agape* love in

*Situation Ethics, Joseph Fletcher. Copyright 1966, Westminster Press, p. 136.

his book *Situation Ethics*. In Fletcher's opinion, seaman Holmes did a "bravely sinful yet good thing." In effect, here is Christian ethics in action.

Few would argue that seaman Holmes did not do the "practical thing." Few would even deny that he was "brave" in the sense that he did what no one else seemed to have nerve enough to do—lighten the boat by throwing several human beings overboard. Whether seaman Holmes did a "good thing" is another matter, which will be discussed later in this chapter. But, for the moment, consider Fletcher's opinion that this was an act of "Christian" love. The Bible teaches that Christians are indwelt and empowered by the Holy Spirit.*

What does Fletcher mean by "Christian"?

On page 56 of *Situation Ethics*, Joseph Fletcher emphasizes that from this point on he will be talking about "Christian" situation ethics. In another writing, Fletcher claims that the new morality is the "true Christian morality." Fletcher's colleague, Bishop John Robinson, agrees that the new morality is definitely a Christian approach. In his book *Christian Morals Today*, the Bishop constantly refers to "Christian ethics." For example, "In Christian ethics, the only pure statement is the command to love. Every other injunction depends on and is an application of it."**

Since Fletcher and Robinson both plainly state that the new morality is "Christian," it is fair to ask

---

*See, for example, I Cor. 2:10-16; John 14:26; Rom. 8:9.
***Christian Morals Today*, Bishop John A. T. Robinson. Copyright 1964, Westminster Press, p. 16.

Everybody has the Holy Spirit—whether they believe in Christ or not.

JESUS SAVES (GREEN STAMPS)

DOWN WITH CHRIST UP WITH MARX

IS THE HOLY SPIRIT IN "ALL MEN"?

them to define their terms. What do they mean by "Christian"?

Although Fletcher does not go into detail on his concept of "What is a Christian?" he gives you a strong clue when he writes in *Situation Ethics* on page 51:

"The Christian situationist says to the non-Christian situationist who is also neighbor—or person—concerned: 'Your love is like mine, like everybody's; it is the Holy Spirit. Love is not the work of the Holy Spirit, it *is* the Holy Spirit—working in us. God *is* love, He doesn't merely *have* it or *give* it; He gives Himself—to all men, to all sorts and conditions: to believers and unbelievers, high and low, dark and pale, learned and ignorant, Marxists and Christians and Hottentots.' "*

Fletcher is simply saying that everyone has the Holy Spirit, no matter what his spiritual condition might be. He is claiming that the Holy Spirit is in everyone, no matter what that person's relationship

*Situation Ethics, Fletcher, p. 51.

is to Christ, no matter what that person's response has been to Christ's sacrifice on the cross for his sins. Fletcher also says that the Holy Spirit is not a person, not the third person of the Trinity, but *love*.

What does the Bible teach about the Holy Spirit?

Fletcher's interpretation of the Holy Spirit is hard to find in the Bible, because it simply just isn't there. The Bible makes it plain that the Holy Spirit is a Person. Christ Himself told the disciples that after He left them they would be given "... another Comforter, and He will never leave you. He is the Holy Spirit, the Spirit who leads into all truth" (John 14:16,17, *Living New Testament*).*

But even more to the point, the entire message of the New Testament is precisely that all men do not have the Holy Spirit, all men do not have God. True, all men are created in the image of God. (See Genesis 1:27.) But, they do not have the Holy Spirit in them because they rejected God and they are doomed forever for their sins. (See Eph. 2:1, *Living New Testament*.)**

The Holy Spirit does work in the heart of the unbeliever, and this work is outlined in John 16:7-11, "And when He has come, He will convince the world of its sin, and of the availability of God's goodness, and of deliverance from judgment" (John 16:8, *Living New Testament*). But "having the Holy Spirit," that is, possessing the power and guidance

---

*For other references containing the personal pronoun referring to the Holy Spirit, see Acts 5:3, Matt. 12:31 and Mark 3:29.
**For Biblical teachings on the universality of sin, see I Kings 8:46; Ps. 53:3; Isa. 53:6; Prov. 20:9; and I John 1:8.

of the Holy Spirit is strictly for the Christian—the person who has received Christ as his personal Saviour and Lord. All who receive Him have the ". . . right to become children of God" (John 1:12, *Living New Testament*). When a person believes in Christ he is "born again": "Men can only reproduce human life, but the Holy Spirit gives new life from heaven" (John 3:6, *Living New Testament*).

The Christian believer has Scripture's promise that the Holy Spirit "shall guide you into all truth . . ." (John 16:13, *Living New Testament*).* The Christian also knows that ". . . the Holy Spirit has been at work in your hearts, cleansing you with the blood of Jesus Christ and making you to please Him" (I Peter 1:2, *Living New Testament*).

Christ's opinion on "All men have the Holy Spirit"

Jesus Christ made it explicitly clear that the non-Christian does not have the Holy Spirit. His famous "bread of life" discourse (John 6) was dedicated to the central theme: It is the Spirit that gives life, and the flesh (the unsaved man's concern with the material and secular) profits nothing. (See John 6:63.) Christ also told His disciples when He promised them the Holy Spirit in John 14:17 that "The world at large cannot receive Him (the Holy Spirit) for it isn't looking for Him and doesn't recognize Him" (John 14:17, *Living New Testament*).

All of these plain statements from Scripture are hard to reconcile with Joseph Fletcher's claim that:

*For Biblical examples of how the Holy Spirit guided believers, see Peter's experience with the messenger sent by Cornelius, Acts 10:19,20; also the account of how Barnabas and Paul received a missionary assignment, Acts 13:2.

"*Your* love is like mine, like everybody's; it is the Holy Spirit. Love is not the work of the Holy Spirit, it *is* the Holy Spirit—working in us. God *is* love . . . He gives Himself—to all men . . . to believers and unbelievers . . ."*

Nor is Fletcher's statement about the Holy Spirit easy to reconcile with Rom. 8:9: "You are controlled by your new nature if you have the Spirit of God living in you. (And remember that if anyone doesn't have the Spirit of Christ living in him, he is not a Christian at all" (*Living New Testament*).

What Paul taught about the Holy Spirit

Paul the apostle deals at length with the difference between the believer and the unbeliever and just what the Holy Spirit does or doesn't do for each. In I Cor. 2:10-16, after mentioning the wonderful things in store for those who love the Lord, Paul says:

"But we know about these things because God has sent us His Spirit to tell us, and His Spirit searches out and shows us all of God's deepest secrets . . . And God has actually given us His Spirit (not the world's spirit) to tell us about the wonderful free gifts of grace and blessing that God has given us . . . But the man who isn't a Christian can't understand and can't accept these thoughts from God, which the Holy Spirit teaches us. They sound foolish to him, because only those who have the Holy Spirit within them can understand what the Holy Spirit means. Others just can't take it in" (I Cor. 2:10-14, *Living New Testament*).

Can the Christian really say to the non-Christian:

---

*Situation Ethics, Joseph Fletcher, Page 51.

Since all men have the Holy Spirit, we don't really need this.

The Gospel
Christ died for our sins

ARE ETHICS WITHOUT THE GOSPEL "CHRISTIAN"?

"Your love is like mine, like everybody's; it is the Holy Spirit"?

As new morality critic Vernon Grounds pointedly observes, to defend the idea that the Holy Spirit operates in all men of good will whether they are Christians or not is to "... set aside the whole New Testament. It is to deny that faith-relationship with Jesus Christ brings about any difference in human lives. It is to render the Gospel a superfluity."*

The "Gospel" that is clearly presented in the New Testament is not some kind of statement about "loving your neighbor responsibly" and making sure that you get into the right organization that is concerned with social action. The Gospel of the New Testament is stated plainly over and over again and is summed up in the words of Paul: "... Christ died for our sins just as the Scriptures said He would, and ... He was buried, and ... three days

*"The New Morality: What's Wrong with the New View of Right?" Vernon Grounds. *His*, November 1967, p. 16.

afterwards He arose from the grave just as the prophets foretold" (I Cor. 15:3,4, *Living New Testament*).

The Gospel means literally "good news." This good news is really bad news in a way for those who think they can "work their way to heaven." The Bible makes it plain: all civic-minded, well-meaning, neighbor-concerned people are not necessarily on God's side. The Bible makes it plain that not all those who sincerely believe in the war on poverty, the Peace Corps or in bringing an end to all wars are bound for heaven. In other words, the "good guys" are not necessarily saved. Paul makes this crystal clear in Romans 2 when he condemns the "ethical and moral" man for his sins right along with the immoral pagans. "All have sinned; all fall short . . ." (Rom. 3:23, *Living New Testament*). That surely includes those who devote their lives to the service of mankind but fail to do business with God about their own sins.

You can't buy a ticket to heaven

You can give away millions to help the poor and the diseased; you can win the Nobel Peace Prize; you can discover the cure for cancer, but that won't "buy you a ticket to heaven."

The good news in the New Testament is that a man can be saved from his sin and his guilt through trusting Christ and this is only made possible through the grace (mercy and kindness) of God. Paul writes to the Christians at Ephesus and tells them: "Because of His kindness you have been saved through trusting Christ. And even trusting is not of yourselves; it too is a gift from God. Salvation is not a reward for the good we have done, so none of us can take any credit for it" (Eph. 2:8,9, *Living New Testament*).

Paul writes in the first chapter of his letter to the Romans that the Gospel is more than good news, it is the power of God Himself. "It is God's powerful method of bringing all who believe it to heaven" (Rom. 1:16, *Living New Testament*).

Does Fletcher teach "universal salvation"?

When Joseph Fletcher writes that all men have the Holy Spirit he is virtually saying that the Gospel isn't necessary. Or, he may be trying to say that because Christ died for the sins of all men, it follows that all men have the Holy Spirit whether they recognize it or not. This second viewpoint is typical of "universalism"—the idea that all men are saved because Christ died for their sins. Not all men realize or understand what Christ did, say universalists, but all men are saved nonetheless.

Universalism is not taught in the Bible. What universalists do is to pluck certain verses out of Scripture and prove their position with these verses. Most of these verses fall into the category of God's *offer* of salvation to all men, which is indeed "universal." In Matt. 24:14 the Lord says that ". . . this gospel of the kingdom shall be preached in all the world . . ." and in Matt. 28:19 He tells His disciples: "Go ye therefore, and teach all nations . . ."*

A favorite text of teachers of universalism (among whom are many neo-orthodox scholars) is I Cor.

*For other verses on the universal offer of the Gospel to all men, see Mark 16:15; Acts 1:8; Rev. 14:6.

15:22, "For as in Adam all die, even so in Christ shall all be made alive." The universalist overlooks two things when using this for a proof that all men will someday be saved: (1) the *context* of the verse —I Cor. 15—which deals with the Gospel Christians have *received and believed in* (see vs. 1 and 2); (2) in Scripture the word "all" is used conditionally according to the passage and what is being said.

Paul says that in Christ all shall be made alive, he means all who shall *believe* in Christ shall be made alive. This is the overwhelming testimony of the rest of the New Testament. You substantiate any doctrine from the Bible by getting the total teaching of the Bible. You do not build a theological position on one or two verses plucked out of context.

But an offer is one thing; accepting an offer and coming to God in repentance for your sins is another. You cannot give a man a gift if he does not take it. God does not force His Gospel on any man. God loves all of us so much that He made us free— free to choose Christ or to reject Him. If God had "forced" all men to believe in Him, if He had manipulated their minds so they would only accept the Gospel, then He would not have men, He would have puppets. Love is a feeling that can only be experienced between persons. The Gospel is offered to persons, it is not forced upon puppets.

Meanwhile, back in that overloaded lifeboat, there is no information on whether seaman Holmes was really a Christian or not. We only have Joseph Fletcher's assurance that "all men have the Holy Spirit," which is hardly a Biblical deduction.

THE GOSPEL IS NOT FOR PUPPETS

With the lifeboat situation, as with almost every situation he cites in *Situation Ethics*, Fletcher reduces Christian ethics to secular ethics or he does not differentiate between the two. This is simply not the teaching of the Bible, and in effect Fletcher takes it upon himself to define in his own terms what he thinks a Christian really is and what he thinks Christian ethics is.

But "being a Christian" either means something or it does not. The Bible makes it clear that a person does not "become a Christian" by being born in the United States or any other so-called "Christian" nation. A person does not become a Christian by being born into a Christian family and being taken to Sunday School and church throughout his childhood years. A person does not even become a Christian by joining a so-called "Christian" church.

The Bible teaches that a person becomes a Chris-

tian when he "does personal business with Christ."
All who receive Christ are given the right to become the children of God (John 1:12). All who
believe on Him will not perish but have everlasting
life (John 3:16).

Believing is done at the "gut level"

What does it mean to believe? It means .more
than just admitting that Christ lived and that He
died for your sins. It means *trusting* in Him, not
only with your head, but at the "gut level" as well.
"For it is by believing in his heart that a man becomes right with God; and with his mouth he tells
others of his faith, confirming his salvation" (Rom.
10:10, *Living New Testament*).

Is situation ethics really "Christian ethics"? It all
depends. It all depends on what you mean by
"Christian" and what you mean when you talk
about the "Holy Spirit." It all depends on what you
see when you read the Bible—God's revealed Word
and will for men or a collection of "moral, ethical
and religious writings by men of another day."

Joseph Fletcher may manipulate words like
"love" and "Holy Spirit" as much as he wishes, but
his opinions do not change the unmistakable teaching in Scripture. The Holy Spirit is *not* in all men
because all men do not know Christ as personal
Saviour and Lord. Indeed, many men openly oppose Jesus Christ, blaspheme His name and figura-
tively spit in His eye. Christ's offer of love to all
men still stands, however, but that offer of love—
even to those who hate Him, disparage Him or
ignore Him—does not mean that all men have the

Holy Spirit. If a man wants the Holy Spirit, he can have Him, but there is a condition. That condition is acceptance of Jesus Christ as Saviour and Lord.

In *Situation Ethics* Joseph Fletcher writes in a way that blurs the meaning of words like Christian and Holy Spirit, but as blurry as these words are, they are not as fuzzy as some of Fletcher's other favorites, such as "responsibility" and "love." The fuzziest word in Fletcher's system is "love" and ironically this is the word on which he bases everything, as you will see in the next chapter.

TAKE TIME . . .

Use the following ideas to take time to apply the Bible to your life and any situation you face.

Front page news or routine want ad?

In *Situation Ethics,* Joseph Fletcher writes that the Christian situationist can say to the non-Christian situationist who is also concerned about persons: "*Your* love is like mine, like everybody's; it is the Holy Spirit. Love is not the work of the Holy Spirit, it *is* the Holy Spirit —working in us."* Compare this thinking with these ideas that Paul offers concerning the Holy Spirit, Christians and non-Christians:

⁹"... no mere man has ever seen, heard or even imagined what wonderful things God has ready for those who love the Lord. ¹⁰But we know about these things because God has sent His Spirit to tell us, and His Spirit searches out and shows us all of God's deepest secrets. ¹¹No one can really know what anyone else is thinking, or what he is really like, except that person himself. And no one can know God's thoughts

Situation Ethics, Joseph Fletcher, p. 51.

except God's own Spirit. [12]And God has actually given us His Spirit (not the world's spirit) to tell us about the wonderful free gifts of grace and blessing that God has given us. [13]In telling you about these gifts we have even used the very words given us by the Holy Spirit, not words that we as men might choose. So we use the Holy Spirit's words to explain the Holy Spirit's facts. [14]But the man who isn't a Christian can't understand and can't accept these thoughts from God, which the Holy Spirit teaches us. They sound foolish to him, because only those who have the Holy Spirit within them can understand what the Holy Spirit means. Others just can't take it in. [15]But the spiritual man has insight into everything, and that bothers and baffles the man of the world, who can't understand him at all. [16]How could he? For certainly he has never been one to know the Lord's thoughts, or to discuss them with Him, or to move the hands of God by prayer. But, strange as it seems, we Christians actually do have within us a portion of the very thoughts and mind of Christ" (I Cor. 2:9-16, *Living New Testament*).

In verse 10 of this passage, what is Paul talking about when he speaks of "us"? For clues, see John 14:17; Rom. 8:9; Eph. 2:1-13.

According to vs. 14 and 15 of this passage, who considers the thoughts of God as foolishness? Can you call the thoughts of God foolishness and still possess the Holy Spirit? Look back to vs. 12 and 13.

Write a short paragraph comparing the work of the Holy Spirit in the believer and the non-believer. Would Paul have said to the non-Christian that "Your love is the Holy Spirit and he works in both of us?" Why? Why not?

Again and again the Bible spells out clearly and distinctly that there is a difference between the believer and the unbeliever, between the saved and the unsaved, between the Christian and the non-Christian. See, for example, John 3:16-18; 5:24; 3:36. As for Fletcher's suggestion that the Bible teaches universalism (he writes in *Situation Ethics* that, "This is the 'saving truth' about themselves which the faithless, alas, do not grasp!"*), the Bible makes it clear that God's offer of salvation is universal. See, for example, Acts 2:21; Rom. 10:13; II Peter 3:9. But God's offer is always based on a condition that men must call upon God, they must repent of their sins, they must receive Christ. To teach that all men are saved but they just don't grasp the idea yet is to make words like sin and salvation meaningless; it is to make the entire Bible somewhat pointless; it is to reduce the Gospel from front page good news to a routine want ad.

TAKE INVENTORY . . .

Are you a Christian? How do you know? Are you depending upon some structure or organization such as church membership? Or are you depending upon your own personal trust in Christ?

If you say you are a Christian, does it affect the way you live? Does it affect your ethics and morals—how you decide between right and wrong? Can you think of any specific examples about how being a Christian affects your daily living?

Think back to the lifeboat situation that Joseph Fletcher describes. What would you have done in the same situation? How would you have practiced "Christian ethics"? Suppose you had been seaman Holmes and the first mate had ordered you to throw some of the men in the boat overboard? Would you have done so? Why? Why not?

Situation Ethics, p. 52.

TAKE ACTION...

Interview several friends and acquaintances and possibly some strangers and ask them this question: "What is a Christian?" See how many of them give answers that revolve around what a Christian does or does not do (doesn't smoke, goes to church, reads the Bible, doesn't swear, etc.).

Do three things this week that are based on your understanding of Christian ethics and morals. Don't wait for something to come up. Actually plan and carry out some project, however small, that is based on your concepts of right and wrong.

Is there anything you can do to improve communications and relations between races in your community or school or place of business? Is there anything you can do in your home to right a wrong or do the right?

Pray about what you decide to do. Does the Holy Spirit seem to be guiding you or is it hard to tell?

CHAPTER 5

My ticket out of prison is getting pregnant, so . . .

How can you know it's really love?

"At the Battle of the Bulge,* a German infantryman named Bergmeier was captured and taken into a prisoner of war camp in Wales. Later, his wife, compelled to forage for food for their three children, was picked up by a Soviet patrol. Before she could get word back to them, she was sent off to a prison camp in the Ukraine.

"Within a few months, Bergmeier was released and upon return to Berlin began the search for his family. He found Paul, who was 10, and Ilse, who was 12, in a Russian detention school. Their 15-year-old brother, Hans, was found hiding in a cellar. But they searched in vain for some word of their mother. Her whereabouts remained a mystery. During those agonizing months of heartache, hunger and fear, they needed their mother to reknit them as a family.

"Meanwhile, in the Ukraine, Mrs. Bergmeier learned through a sympathetic commandant that her husband and children were together in Berlin and were desper-

*World War II, winter of 1944.

ately trying to find her. But the Russian rules would allow her release for only two reasons: (1) an illness requiring medical care beyond the camp facilities, in which case she would be sent to a Soviet hospital elsewhere, and (2) pregnancy, in which case she would be returned to Germany as a liability.

"She wrestled with the alternatives and finally asked a friendly camp guard to impregnate her. When her condition was medically verified, she was immediately returned to Berlin and to her family. They welcomed her with open arms even when she told them how she managed it. When little Dietrich was born, they especially loved him, feeling that he had done what no one else could do—bring the family back together."*

This is one of those "sticky situations" that Joseph Fletcher includes in his book *Situation Ethics* to justify his reasoning that under certain circumstances any act might be right—including adultery. He calls Mrs. Bergmeier's act "sacrificial" adultery and asks if the Bergmeier family was right to feel that little Dietrich was the most wonderful thing that had ever happened to them because he had brought all of them together again. Shouldn't the family even be grateful to the "friendly camp guard"? Fletcher uses this story, which is based on fact, to show that in a certain situation, doing the loving thing might make it necessary to "set aside" that stodgy, stiff seventh commandment, "Thou shalt not commit adultery" (Exod. 20:14).

Before considering Mrs. Bergmeier's case further, it will be helpful to look into just what Fletcher means by these favorite words he uses so often in *Situation Ethics*: "The loving thing."

*Quoted from *The New Morality: A Christian Solution*, William S. Banowsky. Copyright 1968, Campus Evangelism, p. 1.

Love is action, no, it's a characteristic, yet it might also be an attitude . . . Oh, why don't we just call it goodwill?

SITUATION ETHICS GIVES INDEFINITE DEFINITIONS OF LOVE

Since Fletcher makes *agape* love the only absolute in his system of situation ethics, you would think that he would be very definite and clear on what he means by *agape* love. In the foreword to *Situation Ethics*, Fletcher writes: "The word 'love' is a swampy one, a semantic confusion."* Fletcher goes on to give various uses of the word "love": from the kind of love suggested in an ad for an "adults only" movie to such expressions as "I love that hat," or "I just love strawberries." Fletcher insists that when discussing ethics, he is talking about the highest kind of love—God's *agape*.** But as Fletcher proceeds through *Situation Ethics*, his vagueness in defining what he means by *agape* love is astonishing.

Situation Ethics, Joseph Fletcher, p. 15.
**In the Greek there are three words used to define the word "love." *Eros* means sexual or passionate love. *Philia* is equal to friendship. *Agape* is the love attributed to God—the love that asks nothing from the one loved. In the New Testament, only the word *agape* is used when speaking of love.

75

Writing in *His* magazine, Vernon Grounds observes that Fletcher gives almost a dozen definitions for the word love. According to Fletcher, love can be an action, a motive, a principle, or just plain "good will."*

Situation ethics preaches "sloppy 'agape' "

Grounds points out that advocates of the new morality such as Joseph Fletcher and Bishop John Robinson use the word "love" just about any way they want in their writings. At one time they seem to be talking about the self-sacrificing love of Jesus Christ that was shown on Calvary—the true New Testament *agape*, the supreme example of the kind of love that asks no love in return. But at other times they abandon this meaning and slide over into other meanings that are actually much closer to the secular kinds of love, which go on at a human level and fall far below the completely self-giving quality of *agape* love, which originates only with God.

While Joseph Fletcher is fuzzy about what he means by love, he comes on strong when he talks about basing his law of love on Jesus' "summary commandment," given in Matt. 22:37-40 as Jesus and a lawyer have the following dialogue:

"Sir, which is the most important command in the laws of Moses?" Jesus replied, " 'Love the Lord your God with all your heart, soul, and mind.' This is the first and greatest commandment. The second most important is similar: 'Love your neighbor as much as you

*See Vernon Grounds' discussion of this in "The New Morality: What's Wrong with the New View of Right," Part II, *His*, November 1967, p. 24. Also see Fletcher's varying definitions of the word 'love' on pages 60, 61, 63, 79, 104, 105 and 155 of *Situation Ethics*.

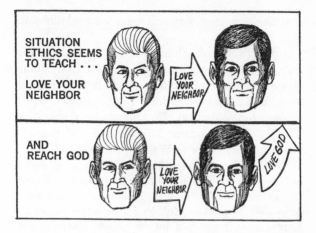

love yourself.' All the other commandments and all the demands of the prophets stem from these two laws and are fulfilled if you obey them. Keep only these and you will find that you are obeying all the others" (Matt. 22:36-40, *Living New Testament*).

Fletcher has a novel approach to interpreting this summary commandment. Throughout *Situation Ethics,* he uses the phrase: "Love God *in* or *through* your neighbor."

Nowhere in Scripture, however, is the phrase "love God in or through your neighbor." What the Bible does say is that God is love (*agape*). See for example I John 4:16. By definition, *agape* love is *not* the act of a human being loving other human beings; it is the act of God loving persons.

William Banowsky, vice-president of Pepperdine College and outspoken critic of the new morality, observes that human beings cannot develop *agape* from within themselves. They can only respond to God's *agape* love for them. The capacity to love someone else, then, depends upon your relationship with God.*

Although Joseph Fletcher seems to realize that love for others must start with love for God,** the overwhelming emphasis in his book is on "neighbor love," and he speaks little of the Christian's direct relationship with God. He continually emphasizes that the Christian must love God in and through the neighbor. C. Peter Wagner, professor of ethics at the Emmaus Bible Institute of Bolivia, observes:

"Love for Fletcher is neighbor love, but this is only the second table of the law. The first is to love God. Jesus said, 'If you love Me, you will keep My commandments.' It is impossible for us to love our neighbor properly without first loving God, and we in turn show our love to God by obeying His commandments. To suppose that a man could first love his neighbor without first loving God is folly."***

The essential difference between Fletcher's situation ethics and Biblical ethics is this: Fletcher says that you love God in and through your neighbor. (The implication is that if you didn't have any neighbors you couldn't love God.) The Bible, however, says that you can't really love your neighbors until you decide to sincerely love God, and receive some of His love to pass on to your neighbor.

*"The New Morality: A Christian Solution," William Banowsky, p. 13.
**On page 49 of *Situation Ethics,* Fletcher states that faith comes first and the Christian understands love in terms of God as seen in Christ. Fletcher quotes Paul's phrase in Gal. 5:6, "faith working through love," as the essence of Christian ethics. But as Fletcher moves through his book, the emphasis switches almost completely to the idea that love for God is involved in loving your neighbor. Fletcher even defines love as good will at work in partnership with reason (p. 69). In effect, his approach to reducing love to concern for persons and neighbors (which sounds so noble) often reverses the Biblical order which says that man first loves God and then is empowered to love his neighbor. Fletcher's emphasis is that man loves his neighbor and thereby loves God.
***Eternity* magazine, February, 1967, p. 59.

THE BIBLE TEACHES: LOVE GOD FIRST,

GOD'S LOVE

LOVING RESPONSE TO GOD

THEN YOUR NEIGHBOR

LOVE BETWEEN GOD AND YOU

LOVE FOR NEIGHBOR

Joseph Fletcher would have you believe that when it comes to ethics and morals, all that counts is love. The Bible, however, teaches that you need love *and* law. One way to picture this is an arch— an arch that leads, you might say, to a correct system of personal Christian ethics.

The blocks that make up the sides of the arch are the Ten Commandments. But, as any builder will tell you, the "keystone" is the all-important item in the arch. Without the keystone the arch will collapse and crumble to the ground. In this illustration (see p. 80), the keystone is the "rock of love." In other words, Jesus' summary commandment to love God with all your heart mind and soul and to love your neighbor as yourself does not do away with all the laws and leave love standing alone unsupported and undefined. In effect, love needs the rocks of the law and the rocks of the law need love in order to complete the entry way to a solid

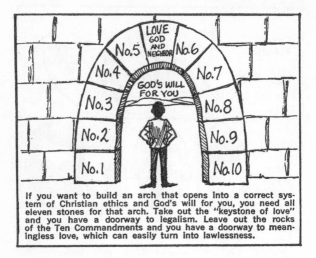

If you want to build an arch that opens into a correct system of Christian ethics and God's will for you, you need all eleven stones for that arch. Take out the "keystone of love" and you have a doorway to legalism. Leave out the rocks of the Ten Commandments and you have a doorway to meaningless love, which can easily turn into lawlessness.

system of Christian ethics. Without love the Ten Commandments crumble to the ground and become legalism. Without the Ten Commandments, love crumbles to the ground as meaningless and undefined. All of the rocks in this arch are needed to complete the arch. The builder cannot set some of the rocks aside and say "Maybe we will use these and maybe we won't."

Every one of the Ten Commandments is sound and solid, and the Ten Commandments fill the supporting sides of the arch, and it is finally summarized or completed in the keystone—the law of love.

Therefore, the Christian faces life realizing that there are plenty of dilemmas and plenty of sticky situations, but he faces these situations by trying to make his ethics harmonize with the moral principles stated in Scripture. As new morality critic William Banowsky puts it, "The reason some moral actions can be branded always wrong and never right is that they are acts which can never be consistent with *agape* (with the absolute law of love)."*

You don't rationalize bad into good

When you start subjectively interpreting right and wrong you might end up with no standard of right or wrong at all. Bad does not become good simply because you want to whitewash it with a thick coating of rationalization.

Good is good and evil is evil and when the Christian has to choose between the "lesser of two evils" he does so by throwing himself on the grace of God and realizing that because of his own sinful fallibility he must always throw himself on the wisdom and resources of God and ask God to bring him through. Then, and only then, will he be able to walk through the arch built by the Ten Commandments and the keystone of love and find his way into a solid system of Christian ethics. Any other direction leads into the slough of situational despond.

Sticky situations that don't have easy answers don't prove situation ethics right any more than an increasing crime rate disproves the value of having a police force. Because some situations are neither black nor white, and because some situations leave you doing the "lesser of two evils" doesn't mean that you can toss out the rulebook.

Picture, if you will, a football (basketball, baseball, or tennis) game with only one rule—fair play.

*"The New Morality: A Christian Solution," Banowsky, p. 15.

SITUATION ETHICS: LIKE PLAYING A FOOTBALL GAME WITHOUT ANY RULES

Or perhaps you would prefer to call this one rule "benevolent, sportsmanlike good will." Fletcher alludes to the analogy of one situationist who claims that the Ten Commandments are like some of the rules of strategy in athletics: "...punt on fourth down," "always take the 3-0 pitch."* The trouble with this analogy is that it talks about "strategy" and not about the real rules of the game.

There is nothing illegal about deciding to run or pass on fourth down. There is nothing illegal about swinging at the 3-0 pitch or throwing a cross-court pass. There are, however, many rules in sports that are unbreakable. In football, some of these rules are: "Thou shalt not clip" (block a man from behind). Another one is: "Thou shalt not rough the kicker" (tackle him while he still has one foot high in the air after punting the ball and thereby quite possibly breaking his leg). Another obvious rule in

*Situation Ethics, Fletcher, p. 28.

football is: "Thou shalt remain onside until the ball is snapped."

If you would try to run athletic games with nothing more than "the rule of love or sportsman-like good will" you would have chaos. There would be far more cheating, fouling and mayhem going on than you could possibly contend with. There would even be far more hypocrisy and phoniness than there would be through the strict legalistic obe-dience to the rules.

Without rules, you have no ball game

To put it simply, if you don't obey the rules in sports, "you have no ball game." The same is true of the "game of life." You have to live the game of life by the rules, not by some vague concept of good sportsmanship or benevolent goodwill. And if you don't live the game of life by the rules, you have no ball game here, either. You have anarchy, glossed over with a sickly sweet coating called "love."

You cannot go into life and "call 'em like you see 'em" according to your own opinions. Any judge in any court will tell you that people "see 'em" much differently when it comes to describing what hap-pened in an accident or just who said or signed what in a contract dispute.

As noble and gallant as the advocate of situation ethics might sound or intend to sound, his system just doesn't fit the game of life. The laws and rules that govern any athletic contest and the laws and rules that govern life (the Ten Commandments) are not to be confused with legalism.

But what about Mrs. Bergmeier?

Still, there *are* those sticky situations—like Mrs. Bergmeier's. Surely her motives to get home to her family made her act of sacrificial adultery with the prison camp guard a good and right thing? But was it really? Was it really a good example of Christian love and Christian ethics?

William Banowsky points out that despite the fact that Mrs. Bergmeier's purpose was certainly very noble, she "... cunningly exploited a fellow human being to serve her purpose. Would situation ethicists really believe that she treated the guard as a person—or a thing? Was the guard a married man? Did he have a family? In her concern for her own family, Mrs. Bergmeier lost sight of love's interest for his family."[*]

Another critic of the new morality and its sticky situation arguments is Vernard Eller, professor of religion at LaVerne College (Church of the Brethren) in LaVerne, California.[**] Eller takes Fletcher's illustration of Mrs. Bergmeier and writes a "few more chapters" in which he modifies a few details but changes nothing that affects the basic ethical issues involved.

Suppose, muses Eller, the woman has become pregnant by the guard and is now free but still some 200 miles away from home and it is winter. Unless she gets food soon, she will starve to death and her original "act of sacrificial adultery" will

[*]"The New Morality: A Christian Solution," p. 19.
[**]See "The Ethic of Promise," Vernard Eller. *Christian Century*, July 31, 1968; p. 965.

have been in vain. And so she comes to a farm house and the farmer offers her food if she will (you guessed it!). If the woman was right to submit to the guard's sexual advances, it follows that in this situation, as she is desperate for food and hungry, it is only right that she submit to the farmer. So she does and gets some food.

The truck driver will give her a lift—IF . . .

Once again she finds herself out on the road and discovers that she can't walk the rest of the way home, she is tired and she will probably freeze to death. A truck driver comes along and offers her a ride *if* . . . Certainly, if her act of "sacrificial adultery" was right with the guard and with the farmer, why not with the trucker?

And so, she finally gets back to a city near the village where her children are. But she suddenly realizes that she has no way to support her children. It is hardly practical to be reunited with her children and then to lovingly starve to death with them.

But enough men are on hand in the city who are also interested in using the woman for sexual purposes. She is soon able to raise a sizeable bank roll. In fact, the size of her bank roll convinces her that by accumulating still greater funds she can demonstrate even more love for her children and provide for them in an even better way. She winds up deciding that the most loving thing that she can do for her children is to stay away from them, continue her new found profession of prostitution and just send her family the checks.

At what point does the story become absurd?

Eller admits that he has reduced Fletcher's example to absurdity, but then he asks an interesting question: *At what point did the story become absurd?* When the farmer wanted sex in turn for food? When the trucker did? When the lady got to the city and decided to become a prostitute in order to make a living? Or did the example really become absurd back in the prison camp when the woman took the first step in a series of immoral actions?

Although these modifications of the Bergmeier story are far fetched and extreme, are they really, at their base, inconsistent with Fletcher's thinking? Are they really any more rare or far out than what Fletcher keeps coming up with in *Situation Ethics* as examples of "sticky situations"?

In the Bergmeier situation, staying in prison would definitely require courage, conviction and trust in God. Committing "sacrificial adultery" to get out of prison might be practical and effective, but hardly something that a professor of ethics should hold up as "right and good."

If Christian ethics means anything, it means more than solving the immediate problem, no matter now noble your intentions might be. Christian ethics by definition, involves Jesus Christ, and this involves responsibility to God Himself.

Jesus Christ did not ignore God's laws. In John 15:10, Jesus says that He Himself has kept His Father's commandments to abide in His Father's love and if His disciples truly loved Him, they would do the same.

The question, then, is what should Christ's disciples (His followers, those who believe and trust in Him) do today?

It all does depend, doesn't it?

TAKE TIME ...

Use the following "take time" ideas to apply the Bible to your life and situations you face.

What is love? If you mean *agape* love—the kind of love that originates with God—these two passages should help give you a better picture:

We can love because He first loved us.

⁹"God showed how much He loved us by sending His only Son into this wicked world to bring to us eternal life through His death. ¹⁰In this act we see what real love is: it is not our love for God, but His love for us when He sent His Son to satisfy God's anger against our sins. ¹¹Dear friends, since God loved us as much as that, we surely ought to love each other too. ¹²For though we have never yet seen God, when we love each other God lives in us and His love within us grows ever stronger. ¹³And He has put His own Holy Spirit into our hearts as a proof to us that we are living with Him and He with us. ¹⁴And furthermore, we have seen with our own eyes and now tell all the world that God sent His Son to be their Savior. ¹⁵Anyone who believes and says that Jesus is the Son of God has God living in him, and he is living with God. ¹⁶We know how much God loves us because we have felt His love and because we believe Him when He tells us that He loves us dearly. God is love, and anyone who lives in love is living with God and God is living in Him. ¹⁷And as we live with Christ, our love grows more perfect and complete; so we will not be ashamed and

embarrassed at the day of judgment, but can face Him with confidence and joy, because He loves us and we love Him too. ¹⁸We need have no fear of someone who loves us perfectly; His perfect love for us eliminates all dread of what He might do to us. If we are afraid, it is for fear of what He might do to us, and shows that we are not fully convinced that He really loves us. ¹⁹So you see, our love for Him comes as a result of His loving us first" (I John 4:9-19, *Living New Testament*).

As you read this passage, what does John tell you about what "real love is"? How does he tell you that you can have this kind of love to give to others?

As you read the passage, do you see anything that would give you the idea that you are supposed to "love God *through* or *in* your neighbor"? Or does the text seem to say that because of your love for God, you will have power to love your neighbor?

Paul's version of the summary commandment

Jesus gave "the summary commandment" in Matt. 22:37-40. Here is another version of it in Paul's words:

⁸"Pay all your debts except the debt of love for others—never finish paying that! For if you love them, you will be obeying all of God's laws, fulfilling all His requirements. ⁹If you love your neighbor as much as you love yourself you will not want to harm or cheat him, or kill him or steal from him. And you won't sin with his wife or want what is his, or do anything else the Ten Commandments say are wrong. All ten are wrapped up in this one, to love your neighbor as you love yourself. ¹⁰Love does no wrong to anyone. That's why it fully satisfies all of God's requirements. It is the only law you need" (Rom. 13:8-10, *Living New Testament*).

According to these verses, are the Ten Commandments set aside? If Paul were not concerned about the

Commandments and if Paul did not believe that they were authoritative rules to guide the Christian, why would he bother to say that if you love others truly you will be obeying all of God's laws and fulfilling all of His requirements? Doesn't this statement then imply that God does have requirements on Christians besides a generalization like "loving others"?

God did not give the law so that legalists could play nit-picking games about what is right or wrong. God gave the law as a framework and as a means to the important end He had in mind, which was love. God first loved men, and as they respond to His love personally then they are capable of loving others. The law, then for a Christian, is not something that snares him in some kind of net called legalism. The law is a means that the Christian uses to love others.

TAKE INVENTORY . . .

Do you consider yourself a "loving person"? What does the term "loving person" bring to mind? Would you say that every Christian has to be a "loving person" to the same degree and in the same way? Why is it that some Christians do not seem very loving at all while some unsaved people seem to be quite kindly and loving? In God's sight, what is more important? A man's response to God's love for him or a man's "loving qualities" that he shows to other people? To put it another way, is the Gospel based on how well we can love, or how well God loved us?

Although all Christians can't be perfectly loving all of the time, they all have potential to be more loving and God works in each believer at the pace that helps that believer grow.

Think of several ways in which you could be more loving. More important, think of people to whom you could show more love.

TAKE ACTION . . .

Sit down and write out three or perhaps half a dozen "loving acts" that you will want to try soon. Remember that a loving act doesn't have to be some time-consuming or highly expensive and extremely difficult thing. Perhaps a loving act for you in the next few days or even in the next ten minutes would be to say hello to a certain person as if you really meant it. Perhaps a loving act for you would be to help someone very close to you by doing some routine chore or nasty little job that this person usually has to do by himself or herself. Perhaps a loving act for you would be to tell someone close to you that you love him or her. Think and pray about it; God will bring many things to mind because God is love.

CHAPTER 6

Anything goes?

The sexual revolution...

Topless (and bottomless) bars ... mini-skirts and mono-kinis ... erotic publications ranging from *Playboy* magazine to hard core pornography and paperbacks that cover every conceivable (and some inconceivable) forms of sexual perversion . . . the power of the "pill" and increasing numbers of pregnant brides ... "co-ed" roommates in the colleges and "noncredit courses" from high school to university level on petting, fornication, and "how to have an abortion without missing a class."

The sexual revolution...

Caused in part by a tradition of Puritan Victorianism that ran smack into the upheaval and chaos of two World Wars ... triggered by a biologist named Kinsey . . . and supposedly welcomed by millions who have thrown off restraints, restrictions

91

and hypocrisy for an honest, mature and "healthy" approach to sex.

The sexual revolution . . .

Some say it's over, that all the old traditions and mores are already dead and the "sexperts" can dance on the graves. Some say that the revolution is still at its height, that we "haven't seen anything yet." Some say it never happened, and that all we're going through now is a "readjustment period."

Sex is alive, is society well?

Whatever your opinion about the sexual revolution, you cannot deny that *something* has happened and it's still happening. It seems that sex is alive, but society is not too well.*

One of the sexual revolution's most widely read pieces of propaganda is *Playboy* magazine, which was founded by its editor-publisher, Hugh M. Hefner, in 1953. Hefner started *Playboy* in that year with $600 of his own money, $6,000 in borrowed funds, and a photo of Marilyn Monroe in the nude.

He parlayed his editorial mixture of sex and the "good life" into a $70,000,000 empire, which now ranks as one of the most successful publishing ventures of all time. In addition to a 37-story office building in downtown Chicago, Hefner also owns "The Mansion," his famous 48-room "pad" on Chi-

---

*Some of the more evident symptoms: publications such as Helen Gurley Brown's handbook on premarital promiscuity, *Sex and the Single Girl;* Ralph Ginzberg's magazine, *Eros,* which was labeled obscene by the Supreme Court; plus an increasing flood of pornographic films, paperbacks, magazines, and photographs that not only make law enforcement agencies and censor boards dizzy, but doubtful about what they can safely label obscene without violating somebody's constitutional rights. See *The Smut Rakers,* Edwin A. Roberts, Jr., National Observer Newsbook, 1966.

cago's near north side, where he beds and boards a special group of "bunnies" (the famous female sex symbols of *Playboy* magazine and the *Playboy* key clubs, which have opened in many major cities in the U. S. and in several foreign countries).

When Hefner printed the first edition of *Playboy*, he didn't date it because he wasn't sure there would be a second. He needn't have worried. The monthly paid circulation of *Playboy* passed 3 million in 1965 and was heading for 5 million by the end of 1968. In addition, *Playboy* has an estimated "pass along" readership of 15 to 18 million, according to the report of an independent study firm.

In addition to *Playboy* magazine, the Hugh Marsten Hefner Enterprises also deal in such *Playboy* products as cuff links, recordings, books, *Playboy* models, a Playboy Theater, TV shows, and even "family resorts" designed with attractions for mother and the children (not just dear old dad).

By standards of financial success, Hugh Hefner, who was working for *Esquire* magazine as a $60 a week copyboy in 1951, has done quite well.

"Playboy" is more than just "girlie pictures"

While it is true that Hugh Hefner sells sex at a tidy profit, it is equally true that *Playboy* is far more than a "girlie book" with pretty women posed in the nude or practically so. *Playboy* is "a point of view," and it is this point of view that has made it successful.

The *Playboy* "point of view" has been described in voluminous and redundant detail by Hefner in what he calls his "Playboy Philosophy," an editorial column which he wrote regularly for the magazine from 1962 to 1966. In the "Playboy Philosophy," Hefner presents "for friends and critics alike *Playboy's* guiding principles and editorial credo." In the first edition of the "Philosophy," Hefner explained how *Playboy's* editorial formula mixes pretty girls (nude and semi-nude) with humor, sophistication, a strong sprinkling of practical philosophy and an impassioned defense of the rights of the individual and the superiority of the American way.

Installment 1 of the "Playboy Philosophy" also spells out Hefner's views of sex. He thinks sex is neither sacred nor profane. He expresses dismay at those who feel that his magazine is obscene because he runs pictures of nude women. He cannot understand why the human body, which is the most remarkable, complicated, perfect and beautiful creation on this earth, can be "objectionable."

"Playboy" archenemy of Puritanism

Hefner claims that those who feel that his magazine is obscene and perverted are the ones who are really sick and perverted because they are shackled by their own puritanical view of sex. "Puritanism" is one of Hefner's favorite themes. Throughout the "Playboy Philosophy" he continually hammers away at America's "puritanical, Victorian hang-ups," which make sex into something evil.*

Playboy Philosophy, Installment 1, pp. 4—6. Puritanism and Victorianism flourished from the 16th to the 19th centuries in England and then America. The Puritans saw sex as a "necessary evil" to reproduce the race and taught that neither the female nor the male should gain any pleasure from the sex act. Victorianism was a neurotic offshoot of Puritanism. Victorians were so sex conscious that they did everything they could to suppress sex or ignore it. Puritanical and Victorian tradition is a major reason for the sexual revolution of the 20th century. For more on Puritanism and Victorianism, see Chapter 7.

Indeed, to hear Hugh Hefner tell it in his "Philosophy," only *Playboy* has the right approach to sex. *Playboy* holds that sex is good, clean fun. Sex is to be enjoyed by all, married or not, says *Playboy*.

Hefner quotes various "experts and authorities" who support his viewpoint. His favorite "prooftexts," perhaps, are the Kinsey reports on the human male and female. Another is psychologist Albert Ellis, who has endorsed premarital sex in lectures before college students.

As Hefner puts it, sex can be an expression of love, but it is not necessarily limited to love only. Sex exists, says Hefner, with or without love, and either way it does far more good than harm.* Hefner comments that he prefers "romantic sex" because he is quite a romantic fellow himself. He

Playboy Philosophy, Hugh M. Hefner. Copyright 1962, 1963, HMH Publishing Company, Installment 1, p. 3.

even assures his readers that he doesn't want them to think he is endorsing promiscuity (one wonders what he thinks he *is* endorsing).

One of the cartoons that appeared in *Playboy* puts Hefner's case quite well. The crew cut young playboy says to the rather rumpled young miss he is passionately embracing, "Why speak of love at a time like this?"

Hefner's revolutionary viewpoints on sex often give people a mistaken idea that sex is about all that he has on his mind, but this is not quite true. His wide open attitudes toward sex go along with his views on life in general. As you read the "Playboy Philosophy," you quickly learn that here is a man who believes strongly in the freedom of the individual to do what he likes. Hefner is a firm believer in free enterprise and the capitalistic system. He is a fearless foe of censorship and other "tyrannies" that squash freedom of speech and other rights guaranteed by the constitution.

"Playboy" crusades are a clever facade

Hefner's "crusades" against the "establishment" and its unfair treatment of the individual are a basic reason why *Playboy* and the "Playboy Philosophy" have the ear (and most certainly the eye) of many college students as well as many others in the "under 25" generation. But *Playboy*'s fight for freedom of the individual is only part of a clever facade. Behind Hefner's solemn claims that he is a misunderstood publisher of a magazine that has a "clean and open view" of sex is a philosophy of life that is potentially far more dangerous to society than pictures of unclad females.

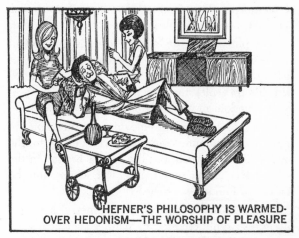
HEFNER'S PHILOSOPHY IS WARMED-
OVER HEDONISM—THE WORSHIP OF PLEASURE

As Hefner himself says, the difference between *Playboy* and its critics *is* rooted in fundamentally opposing views concerning the meaning and purpose of human existence.* Hefner likes to make his critics sound old fashioned, puritanical and full of religious superstition. In turn, he tries to make his opinions and views sound modern, sensible, humane and intelligent.

Actually, Hefner's "Playboy Philosophy" is very old. These same ideas were being taught as early as 400 B. C. by certain Greek philosophers. Hefner, you see, is a hedonist, an "Epicurean-come-lately" who adds a strong dash of American democracy seasoned well with a sharp pinch of laissez-faire capitalism.

As defined by Webster, hedonism is a system of ethics teaching that pleasure is the sole good in life and that moral duty is fulfilled in the gratification

*Playboy Philosophy, Installment 2, p. 2.

of pleasure-seeking instincts. In short, if you are a hedonist, you live for pleasure.

As a philosophy, hedonism includes an ancient and a modern school. The ancient hedonist was strictly egoistic—that is, he was solely concerned with his own pleasure. Among the first teachers of ancient hedonism was Aristippus (435-356 B.C.).

Aristippus believed in enjoying pleasure *now,* to make every minute count in surrendering to the joys of life. For Aristippus the joys of life lay in the senses. His motto was truly, "Eat, drink and be merry, for tomorrow we die."

Ironically, the "eat, drink and be merry" slogan is often mistakenly credited to another ancient hedonist named Epicurus (341-270 B.C.).

Epicurus (who suffered from chronic indigestion) advocated a simple life of meditation, mixed with a diet of bread, cheese and milk, but his main concern was still personal pleasure.

For Epicurus, the "long run" is what counted most. He was the kind of hedonist who counted the cost, and played his cards accordingly, *but always with his own welfare in mind.*

Hedonism's paradox: pleasure is a by-product

The father of modern hedonism was Jeremy Bentham (1748-1832) who put an altruistic touch to the ideas of pain and pleasure. He and his disciple, John Stuart Mill (1806-1873) developed the school of thought called "utilitarianism," which preached the idea of the "greatest good for the greatest number of people."

Henry Sidgwick (1835-1900) followed Mill in the

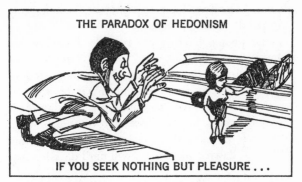

THE PARADOX OF HEDONISM

IF YOU SEEK NOTHING BUT PLEASURE ...

development of a modern hedonistic view, which tried to blend the quest for pleasure with responsible social action. One of Sidgwick's key observations is called the "hedonistic paradox"—the idea that pleasure sought is pleasure lost. Instead of being the be-all and end-all of life, pleasure is really a by-product.

That pleasure is a by-product and not an end in itself is indeed the fly in the hedonist's ointment. Here is the built-in ethical weakness in the hedonistic viewpoint. The hedonist is primarily responsible to no one but himself and his own desire for

POOF

YOU ARE NEVER SATISFIED.

pleasure. He lives for a "by-product," not for any worthwhile, lasting purpose.

Many people have probably never heard of hedonism, but hedonism is still the philosophy they are following in their "pursuit of pleasure." Hedonism is a driving force behind much of what is passing today for the "new morality." Hedonism is a major motive for the "sexual revolution" which advocates premarital and extramarital sex from dark until dawn (and from dawn until dark for that matter).

Hedonists turn from God to themselves

Hedonism—be it with sex, drugs, alcohol, etc.—is a prime example of how human beings can turn from God to themselves. Ironically, in pursuing pleasure on their own terms, they abandon their real source of satisfaction—God Himself. They are left with only themselves—their frustrations, their weaknesses, their greed, their desires. The hedonistic philosopher Henry Sidgwick was never so right: *pleasure sought is pleasure lost.* If pleasure is all you're looking for, your search will never end and you will never be satisfied.

Hugh Hefner does his best to look and sound satisfied. He dresses his *Playboy* philosophy in the latest styles, equips it with a gourmet menu and fast sports car and houses it in a palatial bachelor pad through which wafts romantic stereo music. But, like any brand of hedonism, the *Playboy* philosophy is a pagan point of view, a form of humanism, the worship of man and what man can achieve.

While not claiming to be an atheist, Hefner

makes no pretense to hold any real responsibility to a supreme being and he completely rejects the doctrine of original sin. In fact, a major theme in his "Playboy Philosophy" is the criticism of religion, particularly Christianity, which he sees as a source of some of the worst evils ever to befall mankind.

Hefner's tirade against religion would be amusing if it were not so tragic. Rebelling against his strict religious upbringing, he continually misinterprets or misuses the Bible to "prove his point." For example, while he is sarcastic about Jesus' teachings in the Sermon on the Mount, Hefner has made the statement that if Jesus were alive today and had to choose between a position with *Playboy* magazine or a position on the ministerial staff of a "joy killing, pleasure denying fundamentalist church" he would gladly choose *Playboy*.* In effect, Hefner tries to make it look like "Jesus is on his side" because the Lord was against legalism.

Would Jesus take a job at "Playboy"?

What Hefner fails to mention is that while Jesus was no legalist, He was also no hedonist. In the Sermon on the Mount, Jesus made it clear that the commandment on adultery stood firm, but that behind the letter of the law was the spirit of the law, which went right to the heart of personal purity. That is why Christ said that whoever would even look on a woman with lustful ideas about using her body for his own personal gratification

*Related by William Banowsky in a debate with *Playboy* religion editor Anson Mount before 2000 Texas Tech college students in the Lubbock, Texas auditorium on October 8, 1967. Printed copies of this debate are available from *Christian Chronicle*, Box 4055, Austin, Texas 78751, Cost: 25 cents.

committed adultery with her in his own heart. (See Matt. 5:27-30.)

Jesus also taught that the only real enjoyment in life can come out of being unselfish. He said: "If any man will come after me, let him deny himself, and take up his cross, and follow me. For whosoever will save his life shall lose it: and whosoever will lose his life for my sake shall find it. For what is a man profited, if he shall gain the whole world, and lose his own soul? Or what shall a man give in exchange for his soul?" (Matt. 16:24-26).

Jesus continually talked about self-denial and being willing to settle for something less than materialistic success in order to acquire the "something more" that He had to offer.* By direct contradiction Hugh Hefner claims that any doctrine is evil if it holds that self-denial is preferable to self-gratification. Here is the basic difference between Christianity and *Playboy's* hedonistic "gospel according to Hefner." The Christian does not live to gratify himself, but to glorify God. The hedonist does not live to glorify God but to gratify himself.

"Playboy's" hedonism leads to hyprocrisy

Hefner piously preaches about defending the rights and values of the individual, yet he turns right about and teaches that it's perfectly okay to use individuals (especially female ones) for your own pleasure and your own ends. In fact, *Playboy* magazine makes it clear through its photographs of nude women, its articles and its cartoons and party

*See, for example, Christ's Bread of Life discourse in John 6, which caused a sharp decline in His popularity.

102

jokes that females are to be used whenever and wherever possible, as long as it's all in "good clean fun" and the girl goes along with the gag. That it is a gag, and that the joke is usually on the girl and ultimately on all mankind, is certainly not to be denied. Harvey Cox, author of *Secular City*, put *Playboy* in its proper place when he wrote:

"For *Playboy's* man, others—especially women—are *for* him. They are his leisure accessories, his playthings. For the Bible, man only becomes man by being *for* the other . . . If Christians bear the name of one who was truly man because He was totally for the other, and if it is in Him that we know what God is and we know what life is for, then we must see in *Playboy* the latest and slickest episode in man's continuing refusal to be fully human."*

Whether you want to be the one who uses a woman as a thing, or whether you want to be the woman who is willing to be used as a thing, it is all the same. Whether 18 people agree with you, or 18 million, as estimated by *Playboy*, it is still all the same. The Bible calls it fornication and immorality.

The Christian should also remember that while hedonism offers pleasures for a season in the bedroom, it has skeletons in the closet.

In his "Playboy Philosophy," Hugh Hefner shares a quotation that he memorized in his early teens, a motto that he says helped "shape his life":

"This above all, to thine own self be true and thou cans't not be false to any man."**

But if Hugh Hefner thinks that by "being true to himself" he can be sure he will not possibly be

*Secular City, Harvey Cox. Copyright 1965, MacMillan Co., p. 204.
**See *Playboy Philosophy*, Installment 2, Hugh Hefner. Copyright 1962, HMH Publishing Co., p. 5.

The playboy is naive enough to think that by being true to himself that he cannot be false to anyone else, but responsibility to others runs a poor second to selfishness.

"false to any man," he is being incredibly naive. Shakespeare's line is basically humanism, and not very good humanism at that.* To say that by being true to yourself you won't be false to any man means that you are sure that within yourself is the goodness, fairness and honesty and solid character that will always come to the surface as long as you are definitely living up to all those wonderful virtues that lie within you.

Hefner's quoting of these lines from Shakespeare brings back echoes from *Situation Ethics*, Joseph Fletcher's "new morality." The idea is that man is perfectly capable of always doing the good and loving thing in any situation. All he has to do is exercise his rational mind and sterling character.

*On p. 238 of his book, *The Heart of Hamlet*, (published by Thomas Y. Crowell, 1960) Bernard Grebanier comments that the idea of "To thine own self be true" sounds noble enough—until you realize that in context it can only mean, "Be true to your own material advantage; see to it that you line your pockets well." He sums up the advice of Polonius by saying, "Such guidance will do for those who wish to make the world their prey, but it is dignified by no humanity."

Behind the sexual revolution and the "anything goes" point of view is the attitude: "I want what I want when I want it, and I am going to get it." The "I want it and I'm going to take it" attitude is as old as Adam's first suit of clothes.

But what shall it profit a playboy . . .

Apparently, Jesus would have never made it as a *Playboy* staff writer. Instead of talking abut being true to Himself, He kept talking about being true to God and true to others if you would have others be true to you. He kept quoting little things that Hugh Hefner would undoubtedly call "childish," such as, "For what is a man profited, if he shall gain the whole world, and lose his own soul?" (Matt. 16:26)

Jesus also talked a great deal about man's sin and that He had come to save man from his sin. The Bible clearly and accurately points out that man is a sinner and that the "trouble with man" from Adam onward has been just this: he has been too busy being "true to himself."

Playboy tries to sell its philosophy as a nice, innocent, "All-American" combination of "work hard, but be sure to have plenty of fun." But the only goals of the *Playboy* philosophy are pleasure and self-satisfaction. This might be adequate for animals, but it falls a bit short for human beings.

The trouble with *Playboy's* brand of hedonistic hustling is that life turns into a treadmill. Ironically, the playboy, who has supposedly found freedom from legalism and bothersome moral codes, serves his own particular master: the law of self-fulfillment.

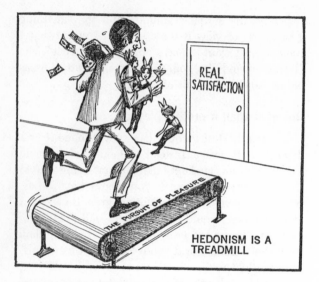

REAL SATISFACTION

THE PURSUIT OF PLEASURE

HEDONISM IS A TREADMILL

One critic of the *Playboy* philosophy writes:

"The playboy is never told, and perhaps Hefner himself doesn't know, how many girls a man has to make before he's got it made. How high must the fi be before it's absolutely right? What cheese do you serve with Burgundy? And what car do you buy when it becomes apparent that the Jaguar is no longer entirely *in*?"*

As Seneca, Roman philosopher of the first century, said, "No man is free if he is slave to the flesh."

It is said that "absolute power corrupts absolutely." It is equally possible that "absolute *pleasure* can corrupt absolutely." Behind Hefner's talk of being true to one's self and assuring the fullest scope to man's individual initiative and competitive na-

*"Come Back to the Garden, Hugh Honey," Jerome Nilssen, *Dialog*.

ture, is the original call of the wild. The words are different, but the melody lingers on: "I'm for me, and everyone else is a potential item on my menu."

Hefner offers his *Playboy* readers a "brave new world" but it easily becomes a jungle. In this kind of jungle the tigers wear the latest cashmere sweaters and the crocodiles are equipped with the finest aqua lungs available, but it is a jungle just the same. The basic law in this kind of jungle is self-fulfillment. And who would argue that there is anything more self-fulfilled than a tiger, crocodile or python that has just feasted on its prey?

But let us face facts. A lot of people may admit that *Playboy* glorifies hedonism, and their answer is, "So what? Kicks are what count." Hefner's hedonism appeals to many because they are willing to pay any price for pleasure, freedom, excitement and —let us not forget the most important "commodity" of all—sex.

It's the "eve of destruction"

A protest song of the mid-60's was entitled "The Eve of Destruction." America and many other western nations stand on the brink of destruction all right, but not necessarily from nuclear bombs. Why should the communists risk nuclear war when they can watch us choke ourselves to death in an orgy of "anything goes"?

"Nonsense," scoff the new moralists. "We are on the threshold of a great new era of responsible moral decision-making." But somehow their assurances get drowned out in the theme song of secular society: "anything goes."

107

When anything goes, everything goes

Anything goes? No society can make that a permanent theme song and survive. *Anything does not go,* because if *anything* goes, *everything* goes: first, personal commitment to God; second, the unique qualities that make us human beings; and third, the very foundations of society itself.

There is a lot of talk today about: "Is the Bible relevant?" The word "relevant" means "applicable to the matter at hand." What is more applicable to the mess we're in than the message in the Bible? The Bible is telling people today what they have always needed to hear: "You are trying to 'save your own life.' You are trying to make your own life as comfortable and pleasurable as possible, but in your selfish, proud rejection and flight from God, you are not saving your life, you are *losing* it. You are losing it to being a slave to your own desires and habits."

But the Bible offers another way. Instead of urging you to save your life, the Bible offers you an opportunity to "lose your life." "Lose your life?" Yes, that's what Jesus Himself said (Matt. 16:25), and He didn't mean some stupid, suicidal flight from reality. What Jesus meant was to pour your life into glorifying God. The Christian who pours his life into glorifying God does not experience the "hedonistic paradox"—pleasure sought is pleasure lost. On the contrary, the Christian discovers that through a right relationship to God in Christ, pleasure is only one of the many by-products (blessings) that he receives.

Playboy and the rest of the hedonistic herd are

selling society a false bill of goods by making it look as though you have to choose between enjoying sensual pleasure or suffering in the suffocating bonds of "religion." But God is not against competition, or pleasures, enjoyment, joy or fun.

What God *is* against is selfishness and pride, which are at the roots of sin. Sin is what destroys a person and doesn't allow that person to be what God intended him to be. Sin separates man from God.

The choice is basic and we all have to make it: self-centered pleasure seeking or losing your life for Christ's sake. Jim Elliot, missionary martyred by the Auca Indians, put it like this:

"He is no fool who gives what he cannot keep to gain what he cannot lose."

Playboy says:

"Don't be a religious fool. Keep your life for yourself. What have you got to lose?"

Who's right?

It all depends . . .

TAKE TIME . . .

Use the following ideas to take time to apply the Bible to your life and any situations you face. Was Jesus against pleasure?

In his "Playboy Philosophy," Hugh Hefner flatly states that any teaching that suggests that self-denial is preferable to self-fulfillment is sick and evil. Yet, the Bible records that Jesus told His disciples: "If anyone wants to be a follower of Mine, let him deny himself and take up his cross and follow Me. For anyone who keeps his life for himself shall lose it; and anyone who loses his life for Me shall find it again. What profit is there if you gain the whole world—and lose eternal life? What can be compared with the value of eternal life?" (Matt. 16:24-26, *Living New Testament*).

If Hugh Hefner is right, then Jesus is teaching "evil doctrine." What do you think Jesus means? Do you think Jesus is a killjoy and against all pleasure? Or is Jesus saying that there is more to life than self-gratification and looking out only for yourself? (See John 10:10; Eph. 3:14-21; II Cor. 9:8.)

What, basically, is Christianity to you? A way of getting something for yourself or a way to give of yourself and receive far more in return? (See John 6:27-35.)

For more teaching from Scripture of self-denial in Christianity, see Luke 14:26-35; Luke 18:29,30; I Peter 2:11; 4:2. Use a modern translation if possible to get at the meaning of terms like "fleshly lusts."

TAKE INVENTORY . . .

Compare secular ideas on seeking pleasure with the Bible's teachings on how the Christian finds real self-fulfillment. With so much stress today on personal gain and self-satisfaction, is the Christian foolish to live according to the teachings of Christ? Is being a Christian "worth it" to you? Why?

TAKE ACTION . . .

Talk to your friends and acquaintances and ask them these questions: "What is the purpose of life? For what are most people living? For what are you living?" Answers from unbelievers will often center in the idea of living for self, getting all you can while you can, etc.

Then, ask them if the words of Jesus Christ seem to make any sense: "If any man will come after me let him deny himself, and take up his cross, and follow me. For whosoever will save his life shall lose it: and whosoever will lose his life for my sake shall find it. For what is a man profited, if he shall gain the whole world, and lose his own soul? Or what shall a man give in exchange for his soul?" (Matt. 16:24-26).

Assure your interviewee that you are not "trying to convert him," but you are interested in what he thinks of one of Christ's basic teachings. As you converse together, it is quite possible that you may strike a spark of interest in spiritual things. Even if the interest isn't apparent, you will gain a much clearer picture of what your Christian faith really means to you.

CHAPTER 7

Puritans, playboys and prophets

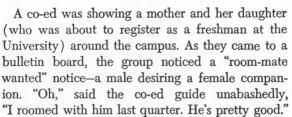

A co-ed was showing a mother and her daughter (who was about to register as a freshman at the University) around the campus. As they came to a bulletin board, the group noticed a "room-mate wanted" notice—a male desiring a female companion. "Oh," said the co-ed guide unabashedly, "I roomed with him last quarter. He's pretty good."

No one knows for sure how many male and female students are living together in off-campus apartments and the like, but this co-ed is no isolated case. Thousands of couples in colleges and universities throughout America are rooming together. Some even claim, "It's great preparation for marriage."

This wide-open attitude toward sex is certainly not limited to the college campus. There is plenty of activity at the high school level and even in the junior highs. Studies reveal that two out of five brides today are teen-agers (average age 18). Fifty percent of teen-age brides are pregnant at the altar. If they are marrying teen-age boys, the figure jumps to 80 percent.*

Wife swapping: a new game for adulterers

And so it goes among the younger generation, who have been quick to learn promiscuity from their parents. Gaining popularity in the decade of the 60's was the pastime of "wife swapping."

"I feel so superior to squares," said one swapped wife. "I know that what we're doing is more open and honest than what millions of husbands and wives are doing . . ."**

Biblical morality is under attack from all sides. Peddlers of the "new sexual freedom" are now trying to tell the world, "You have it all wrong. *We* aren't the ones who are sick. *You* are sick. You are all hung-up because of your puritanical Victorian background. There is nothing really wrong with adultery, fornication or sex outside of marriage, as long as it is done responsibly and as long as no one 'gets hurt'."

Articulate foe of Puritanism is Hugh Hefner, editor-publisher of *Playboy* magazine. Hefner claims that religious Puritanism infects the sexual lives of Americans and that society is guilt-ridden be-

*The Pill and Its Impact, National Observer Newsbook, Robert Ostermann and Mark R. Arnold. Copyright 1967, Dow-Jones and Co., Inc., p. 65.
**EP New Service, July 27, 1968, p. 1.

cause it associates sex with sin.* In many installments of his "Playboy Philosophy," Hefner refers to "Puritanism" and lays this label on anyone who disagrees with his views.

Puritanism originated hundreds of years ago. The label "Puritan" was given to zealous Protestants living in 16th century England. The Puritans wanted to "purify" the Church of England, which they felt had not gone far enough in breaking with the Roman Catholic church during the Reformation, which began in 1520.

The Puritans were persecuted and penalized for their trouble. They fled to Holland and lived there until 1620. Then one group of Puritans sailed on the *Mayflower* for the English colony of Virginia. How they were blown off course to land as Pilgrims at Plymouth Rock in Massachusetts is one of the best known stories of early American history.

The Puritans were austere, earnest and iron-disciplined. Suspicious of any comforts or pleasures which might undermine their spirituality, the Puritans originated rules and regulations of all kinds. Their Sunday blue laws would have made even the Pharisees of Jesus' day nod with approval.

The Puritans were especially suspicious of anything that resulted in pleasure or fun. Their approach to such things as clothing or architecture of buildings was colorless and bleak.**

Their concept of sex was even "bleaker." They saw sex as strictly something to preserve the race.

---

*"Playboy Philosophy," Installment 8, p. 1.
**Although the Puritans were strict and legalistic, there are historians who point out that they weren't complete prudes. See *Sex and the Single Eye*, Letha Scanzoni, Zondervan, 1968, p. 34–36.

According to the Puritans, if a person—male or female—enjoyed sex, that person was considered sinful and "full of lust."

Out of Puritanism came Victorianism, a fanatic, actually neurotic, approach to suppressing sex. For the Victorians, the less said about sex the better. They tried to clothe themselves (especially the women) as completely as possible. They actually made it taboo to even mention things like "legs" or other parts of the anatomy.

Victorianism produced frustration, hypocrisy, and a perverted view of human sexuality. It reached its ultimate in absurdity with such practices as clothing the legs of pianos in "modest" trousers and having little old ladies expressing real apprehension about sleeping in rooms with paintings of men on the walls.

Admittedly, Puritanism and Victorianism produced their share of perversion, hypocrisy and just plain stupid ideas concerning the true nature of sex. Hugh Hefner loves to link these excessive and twisted views of sex with the Christian church, and, of course, he implicates the Bible in his indictment as well.

While Hugh Hefner has little use for Holy Scripture, he often quotes as "holy writ" the highly questionable statistics in the Kinsey reports. Dr. Alfred Kinsey, a zoologist, made a successful study of gall wasps by use of statistical methods. He decided that he would make a study of the sexual behavior of the human male and female in the same way.

According to the Kinsey reports, while Americans supposedly flew the flag of chastity, a great deal of sexual hanky-panky had been going on for a long time.

For his *Sexual Behavior in the Human Male* (1948), he and his staff interviewed 5,300 men on every conceivable sexual subject from masturbation to petting, from homosexuality to premarital and extra-marital intercourse.

For his report on *Sexual Behavior in the Human Female* (1953), he and his staff interviewed 5,940 women on the same subjects.

Kinsey took Gallup Poll approach

Using the "Gallup Poll approach" Kinsey took the results from his small samplings and went on to make generalizations that were supposed to apply to all the other men and women in the country at that time (well over 100 million). The result was that a large portion of the general public accepted his figures as accurate and as a true picture of sexual behavior in American society.

Especially interesting to many people were such figures as 85 percent of the total male population and about 50 percent of the total female population had engaged in premarital intercourse. Kinsey's reports were, in their way, the "shot heard 'round the world." The sexual revolution now had its own "inspired scriptures," its own "proof" that the old morality and the Biblical traditions were no longer being observed and therefore no longer valid.

Kinsey's report is full of weaknesses

What a great many people did not think about were the following weaknesses in the Kinsey report:

Did everyone interviewed by Kinsey and his assistants tell the truth? The interviewees were volunteers, many of whom could have "stretched the truth a bit" to make a good story.

Suppose they had told the truth. Was Kinsey's sampling large enough to build any sound generalization regarding the millions of people in the country? The uncontrolled interview method is not a sound scientific approach, as any scientist will admit.

Perhaps the most serious problem caused by the Kinsey reports was the treatment of the word "normal." Dr. Kinsey took his statistics (obtained, remember, from a very small portion of the male and female populations) and equated the average scores with what he considered to be "normal." Kinsey proceeded to pronounce judgment on tradi-

tional morality (something he had no business doing as a scientist) because his average figures
showed that premarital sex, for example, was far
more "normal" than chastity.

According to Kinsey's reasoning, biological statistics are what would determine moral conduct and
behavior.*

Despite all the weaknesses in the Kinsey statistics,
Hugh Hefner turns to them again and again to
"prove" that the United States is a sexually hypocritical society because traditional American sexual
behavior has been based on Puritanism and Victorianism.**

Furthermore, infers Hefner, because Puritanism
and Victorianism are linked to the ideas that came
out of teachings by the Christian church, this
means that Christianity is suspect and so is the
Biblical view of morality.

Partly right, all wrong

Hefner's arguments are convincing to some (especially among the "under 25 generation") because he
is partially correct. Today's society does show the
effects of puritanical and Victorian hang-ups. There
is a great deal of hypocrisy when it comes to sex.
Certain kinds of sex education still contain the
"scare theme" that seems to forbid sex on the
grounds that it is wrong, evil, dirty, lustful, "not in
good taste," etc. In criticizing these hang-overs
from Puritanism and Victorianism, Hugh Hefner is
absolutely right.

*Christianity and Sex, Stuart Babbage. Copyright 1963, Inter-Varsity
Press, p. 46.
**"Playboy Philosophy," Hugh Hefner, Installment 8, p. 3.

But where Hugh Hefner is absolutely wrong is in linking puritanical and Victorian ideas on sex to Biblical morality. He continually talks about "what the church has taught" and how the "church has made mistakes and committed crimes against humanity." But the mistakes of Christians and the teachings of the Word of God are two different things. The question is not whether Christians have always been correct, but have Christians (such as the Puritans) used the Bible correctly?

The Christian who takes the trouble to find out what the Bible really teaches about sex knows that sexuality is the gift of God, a gift that man is responsible to use correctly.

What does the Bible say on sex?

In I Cor. 6:13, the Apostle Paul completely contradicts *Playboy's* idea that sexual behavior is like drinking a glass of water or having a good meal. Paul points out that human beings are more than bodies with physical desires and appetites. Every person is basically made for God, and that includes a person's sex drive as well as all other parts of him. Every person will find the answer to all of his needs and desires (including the sex drive) through loving and obeying God.

As J. B. Phillips translates I Cor. 6:13: "You cannot say that our physical body was made for sexual promiscuity; it was made for God, and God is the answer to our deepest longings" *(Phillips Translation)*.

In I Cor. 6:14,15, Paul stresses that the Christian believer is a "part of Christ Himself." Certainly no

We know the Bible forbids prostitution, my pet, but does it really say anything about couples like us?

FORNICATION IS NOT LIMITED TO PROSTITUTION

Christian would contaminate the body of Christ by joining part of that body (the believer himself) to a prostitute.

But hold on here. With today's typical couple the girl certainly doesn't see herself as a prostitute (someone who is selling her body for money). Does this mean, then, that Paul is forbidding prostitution, but it's all right to pet and even "go all the way" before marriage as long as you are "in love" and you know you will get married someday anyway?

This is a valid question. It is so valid that some advocates of the new morality claim flatly that the Bible does not teach anything specific in the area of premarital sex. The Christian has to search the Scriptures and make up his own mind.

In the *Phillips Translation,* I Cor. 6:18 warns us to "avoid sexual looseness like the plague!" Over and over again the Scriptures forbid fornication (I Thess. 4:3-5; Col. 3:5; Eph. 5:3-5). Webster defines fornication as a lot more than patronizing a house of prostitution. Fornication means: "(1) human sexual intercourse other than between a man and his wife; sexual intercourse between a spouse and an unmarried person; sexual intercourse between unmarried people."

The Greek word for fornication is *porneia* (and this is where we get our word pornography). There is little question that when the Biblical writers use words like *porneia* they are referring to acts that are immoral, unlawful, and sin in God's sight. Christians are to avoid *any kind* of sexual looseness, *any kind* of fornication, *any kind* of premarital or extramarital sex.

The reason for this commandment from God is plain. God's word teaches that sex is rightly used when there is a genuine and definite commitment between both parties, a commitment in which they place themselves before God in responsible marriage. Any other kind of sex—casual, with love during engagement, without love, and "strictly for recreation," etc.—is sin.

It might be possible to "have no guilt"

Some of the people engaging in premarital and extramarital sex today continue to do a lot of talking about how they "have no guilt." This might be possible for some people. You can sear your conscience and "harden your heart" to the point where you can do just about anything.

For example, there were certain people during World War II who found it quite easy to gas millions of human beings "with no regrets." There are plenty of people who can be hired to kill other human beings and they claim they "have no guilt."

The question is not, "What are some, or even many people, in our society doing?" The question is "What is God's moral law?" Why did God not only pronounce laws concerning morals, but why did He stamp them right into human personality?

While Paul lived before the days of modern psychology and psychiatry, he was well aware that the act of sexual intercourse is far more than a physical one. Contrary to the teachings of playboys like Hugh Hefner, sex is far more than "drinking a glass of water."

William Banowsky, vice-president of Pepperdine College, makes the following observation of sex in one of his criticisms of the new morality:

"Sexual intercourse involves more than the body; it involves the whole person, or shall we more precisely say that it always involves *two* whole persons. Whether they *give themselves wholly* to one another is one thing, but that they are *wholly involved* is beyond doubt."*

It is because of the deep psychological meaning of sex that every Christian should recognize its power. The Christian is responsible to control this power—his sex drive—according to God's rules, not fuzzy concepts of "loving each other responsibly with good clean fornicating fun."

Hugh Hefner may proudly boast in his *Playboy* philosophy about how much good sex can do (from his viewpoint, especially premarital and extramarital sex) but his trumpet makes an uncertain sound.

*"The New Morality: A Christian Solution," William S. Banowsky. Copyright 1968, Campus Evangelism. Published by R. B. Sweet Company, Inc. See pp. 17, 18. Banowsky debated Anson Mount, *Playboy* religion editor, on December 8, 1967 before 2,000 on the difference between Christianity and *Playboy's* hedonistic and humanistic philosophy.

If premarital and extramarital sex do people "so much good," it is strange that there hasn't been more proof of this.

But suppose a "completely playboy society" were organized? In this playboy society premarital and extramarital sex would not be illegal, they would simply be a part of life. People would satisfy their sex drive with the same ease that they satisfy their hunger and thirst.

The Russians have already tried "free love"

Well, it's already been tried, and in of all places, Russia. In his book, *The Great Sex Swindle*, John W. Drakeford includes a chapter on "a sexual utopia" that describes the great "free love" experiment undertaken by Soviet Russia when Communism swept into power in 1917.

A series of Communist decrees brought a complete change in Russian society. All religious concepts were abandoned, along with all religious ideas on sex, marriage and family life. Marriage became a civil contract involving a simple registration, but it was "lawful and legal" even without this formality.

Abortion was legalized and adultery, bigamy and incest ceased to be crimes. Although the Communist government frowned on free enterprise, it literally forced its people into "free love."*

And so, lust had full sway in Russia. Telling themselves that their new worker's paradise was utopia itself, the Russians joyously engaged in for-

The Great Sex Swindle, John W. Drakeford, Broadman Press, 1966, pp. 78, 79. "Free love" is a complete misnomer. Unrestrained sex is not love and it is certainly not free—someone always pays.

Comrade, is finding free love to be capitalist trick. RETREAT!!

THE RUSSIANS DISCOVERED
THAT FREE LOVE ISN'T FREE

nication, adultery, and just about any other sexual act they wanted to try.

What happened?

It seems that sex reigned supreme, but not over paradise. Sexual freedom turned to anarchy. Because a woman became the rightful property of any man who wanted to claim her, the family relationship deteriorated. Parent-child relationships hit a low ebb. The whole thing resulted in chaos. There was nothing to hold a community together.

Sex, far from being a benevolent and just leader, turned into a dictatorial tyrant that ruled an immoral and chaotic empire filled with people on the prowl for sexual pleasure and hordes of parentless bastards who were products of that prowling.

The Russians got the point. They decided that uncontrolled sex and free love were just a little more than they could handle. They halted their head-long charge into unchastity and engaged in what they called "the great retreat."

From Moscow in the middle 1930's came decrees that made divorce, once a routine operation, extremely difficult. Abortion was outlawed. Tax exemptions were offered for large families.

The Russians suddenly decided that lust was no longer a "good bed fellow for atheism." It wasn't that the communists had suddenly "gotten religion." They still rejected all forms of religion, and of course, they still do. The reason they rejected free love was strictly scientific. They tried wide-open sex and it didn't work. Ironically enough, today atheistic Russia has a higher standard of sexual morality than the United States where over 60 percent of the population claims church membership.

Despite *Playboy's* promotion of dishonest, uncommitted sex, Hugh Hefner tries to sound as if he is the archenemy of hypocrisy. He claims that he would have made an excellent psychiatrist because he can see in his critics a "pathological bias against healthy sex." Hefner finds the "sexual hang-ups" of Americans very interesting.*

Hefner's parents taught him rigid religion

When it comes to "psychological hang-ups," it might be interesting to look into Hugh Hefner's own background and childhood. Hefner is the product of a devout Methodist mid-west home. As a teenager, Hefner chafed under rigid "puritanical" ethics: no drinking, no smoking, no swearing, no movies on Sunday. Sex was considered something horrible that was never mentioned.**

*"Mr. Playboy of the Western World," Calvin Thompkins. *Saturday Evening Post,* April 23, 1966, p. 100.
**"Czar of the Bunny Empire," Bill Davidson, *Saturday Evening Post,* April 28, 1962, p. 35.

It is no wonder, then, that Hefner relishes his role as sexual rebel and critic of Christianity. He thumbed his nose at the moral strictures he knew as a child and even had the satisfaction of putting his father, an accountant, on the *Playboy* payroll.*

But in rebelling against his puritanical upbringing, Hefner also tosses out Biblical morality (which Puritanism is *not*). What Hugh Hefner doesn't seem to recognize is that he faces the same kind of paradox experienced by every human being. People want freedom but they need control. People have consciences and when they violate the principles of moral law, sooner or later they run into conflict, guilt, etc. Men and women are made in the image of God, that is why even the most secular men or women still have a sense of right and wrong built into them so that they know what is fair and what is unfair.

Hefner certainly has a sense of what he thinks is fair and unfair. He rips into a society that has weighted him down with what he thinks is an overbearing load of sexual restrictions. As an alternative, he suggests a "fair system" where the man can use the woman for his own pleasure but discard her (gently of course) when playtime is over.

Playtime and pleasure are very important to Hugh Hefner. So is sex. The theme song that

*For a revealing look into Hefner's background, see "A Conservative Looks at Playboy," Lillian Harris Dean. *Christian Herald*, September, 1968, p. 66. Mrs. Dean did an in-depth study of *Playboy* that included a personal visit to Hefner's mansion, as well as a personal interview with Hefner's parents. Hefner's mother holds liberal views, such as seeing the Bible as full of contradictions and believing that a person can be a Christian without believing in the deity of Christ. Hefner's father is conservative, believes in the deity of Christ, inspiration of Scripture and the sinfulness of man.

THE BANDWAGON
ARGUMENT:
OLDEST AND WEAKEST
THERE IS

Hefner wants his *Playboy* readers to sing is, "What the world needs now is sex, sweet sex." Everybody needs sex, everybody wants sex, says *Playboy*. Necking, petting, going "all the way"—everybody's doing it so why not get on the bandwagon?

The "bandwagon" argument that "everybody's doing it" is a favorite tool for promoting sexual immorality today. The idea is that "if you want to be in, popular, accepted, hip, where it's happening, then come on with us and get on the sexual roller coaster." Fornicate and commit adultery to your heart's content, as long as you "do it responsibly and keep it your own business."

As long as the Christian uses his brains and not just his libido, the bandwagon argument has more holes than the proverbial Swiss cheese.

But when a Christian "loses his wits" (and his cool) and lets emotion take over, he's in trouble. Being popular, being accepted, being one of the "in-crowd" becomes more important than what he knows is sensible, logical and what God wants him to do.

Today in America (as well as in other countries around the world) the Christian is bombarded and pressured constantly to adapt a moral code of the secular society. His only hope for resisting this kind of pressure is the sheer re-creative power of Jesus Christ. As Bible scholar William Barclay has said, "The power of Christ is still the same. No man can change himself, but Christ can change him."*

New morality leads to mental hospitals

Playboys and playgirls assure the world that they have outgrown all those puritanical and prudish ideas on sex. They continually try to convince themselves that they are living life to the hilt as mature and responsible members of a society that is seeking a new level of honesty and openness. And, right along with these self-assured claims come reports from reputable psychiatrists that premarital and extramarital sexual relations, growing out of the so-called new morality, have greatly increased the number of young people in mental hospitals.**

New moralities and sexual revolutions come and go, but the image of God is stamped deep within all of us. It is like a mirror. While we might tarnish and cloud it for a time, there are always those inevitable moments when it reflects back what we really are, and those are the moments that make us know that we are incomplete without Christ.

*Letters to the Corinthians, translated and edited by William Barclay, Westminster Press, 1964, p. 60.
**This was the opinion of Dr. Francis J. Braceland, editor of the American Journal of Psychiatry and former president of the American Psychiatric Association while speaking before the National Methodist Convocation on Methodist Theology in 1967. Quoted from Presbyterian Journal, May 3, 1967, "Psychiatrist Notes New Morality Cost."

The Bible doesn't forbid fornication because the Biblical writers were against the joys and pleasures of life. The Bible forbids fornication because God does not want people to be used as things instead of being treated as persons. God does not want people to be cheated, taken advantage of.

Above all, God does not want the most intimate of human relationships to be entered into dishonestly, without full and responsible commitment. God does not want sex to be made into an idol that is worshipped by people who put personal appetite ahead of anything and anyone else.

Sex too fine to waste in fornication

God is not some "all powerful Puritan in the sky" trying to hunt down everyone who might enjoy sex. On the contrary, sex was God's idea in the first place.

God wants men and women to enjoy sex, but they can't enjoy it in its fullest potential if they rob themselves by substituting the cheapness and shallowness of a premarital sexual episode (and it *is* an episode, not a lasting relationship) for the love, security, companionship and warmth of sex as God planned it. "Marriage is honourable in all, and the bed undefiled: but whoremongers and adulterers God will judge" (Heb. 13:4).

"Well," some might say, "since God is going to be judging those who are petting and fornicating and such, that means I've gone too far and there is no hope for me." That is exactly what the Bible does *not* mean. As Jon Braun, former field coordinator of Campus Crusade for Christ, puts it:

"No matter what you've done or how often you've

done it, God will forgive you completely. He is eager to forgive you if you are willing to admit your sin and trust Him ... Further, in His forgiveness, He will restore to you the potential for a happy home, love and marriage ... a completely new start."*

There are many things in life that can bring pleasure and enjoyment, such as fire. But if used in excess or in the wrong way, fire brings pain, destruction, and even death.

Sex is a pleasure of life that can be compared with fire. *Playboy* magazine preaches a "gospel" that says "Enjoy all the fire you want, it won't hurt you a bit." But *Playboy* is wrong. A man much more experienced in matters of sex than Hugh Hefner was King Solomon. Solomon was speaking of sex and lamenting his own immoral use of this wonderful gift of God when he wrote, "Can a man hold fire against his chest and not be burned?"**

There are three basic approaches to sex, and you have to decide which one you want to take: the prudishness of Puritanism? the perverted pleasure seeking of *Playboy?* or the approach revealed by the prophets—the writers of Scripture who teach that sex is good when used according to the will and intentions of the One who created sex in the first place.

The choice is yours. It all depends.

TAKE TIME ...

Use the following ideas to take time to apply the Bible to your life and any situations you face.

Does the Bible really prohibit premarital sex? Some

---

*"What Is This Thing Called Love?" Jon Braun, *Collegiate Challenge*, Vol. 6, No. 2, p. 6.
**Proverbs 6:27, *Living Psalms and Proverbs*, Paraphrased.

people ask the question: "Where in the Bible can you show me that it's wrong to have intercourse with someone I love, especially if we plan to be married soon anyway?"

Read the following passages, and keep in mind that when Paul wrote these letters to first century churches, there were plenty of people going through the frustrations of being sexually attracted to one another, but not yet ready or able to marry. That is why Paul wrote:

"Run from sex sin. No other sin affects the body as this one does. When you sin this sin it is against your own body" (I Cor. 6:18, *Living New Testament*).

"Let there be no sex sin, impurity or greed among you. Let no one be able to accuse you of any such things. Dirty stories, foul talk and coarse jokes—these are not for you. Instead, remind each other of God's goodness and be thankful. You can be sure of this: the kingdom of Christ and of God will never belong to anyone who is impure or greedy, for a greedy person is really an idol worshiper—he loves and worships the good things of this life more than God" (Eph. 5:3-5, *Living New Testament*).

"Away then with sinful, earthly things; deaden the evil desires lurking within you; have nothing to do with sexual sin, impurity, lust and shameful desires; don't worship the good things of this life, for that is idolatry" (Col. 3:5, *Living New Testament*).

"For God wants you to be holy and pure, and to keep clear of all sexual sin so that each of you will marry in holiness and honor—not in lustful passion as the heathen do, in their ignorance of God and His ways. And this also is God's will: that you never cheat in this matter by taking another man's wife, because the Lord will punish you terribly for this, as we have solemnly told you before. For God has not called us to be dirty-minded and full of lust, but to be holy and clean. If anyone refuses to live by these rules he is not disobeying the rules of men but of God who gives His *Holy* Spirit to you" (I Thess. 4:3-8, *Living New Testament*).

For other references on sexual impurity, see Rom. 1:24; 6:19; Eph. 4:19; Heb. 13:4; II Peter 2:10. For verses that talk about lust, see Rom. 13:4; Gal. 5:16; II Tim. 2:22; James 1:15; I Peter 2:11. These are only a few of the Bible's teachings concerning premarital sex and all of the attitudes and desires involved. Anyone can easily see for himself what the Bible teaches. Every person is free to reject or accept what the Bible says, but he should not "Mickey Mouse around" trying to find excuses for fornicating from Scripture . . . they just aren't there.

TAKE INVENTORY . . .

Analyze this statement: "I see nothing wrong with sexual relations prior to marriage as long as we are mature enough to accept the responsibility, it is in love, and no one is hurt."

Many young couples who say they want to engage in sexual relations before marriage (or just plain without marriage) say they are ready to take the responsibility for what will happen. Are *you* ready to take such responsibility? Remember that the "responsibility" may include anything from the birth of another human being (the "pill" does not bat .1000—as you will see in the next chapter) to severe psychological and spiritual depression on the part of your partner if not yourself. (Somebody *can* get hurt.)

Hugh Hefner recommends what he calls "casual sex." By this, he means that it is perfectly all right to enter into the most intimate of personal relationships—sexual intercourse—with no real commitment to the other person. Can you enter into the most intimate of relationships with another person on a casual and "uncommitted" basis? Why?

TAKE ACTION . . .

If you are dating someone rather steadily and have been facing sexual temptations and frustrations, discuss what you have read in this chapter openly with the other person. Are you both aware of the tremendous responsibilities involved in being persons and possessing sexuality?

Are you spending more and more time alone with one another and finding it harder and harder to have a good time when with other people? Are you doing more and more heavy necking and petting but enjoying it less? Ironically, as couples get more and more intimate in a premarital situation, they find themselves growing irritable with one another and drifting apart. Perhaps the answer for many a couple with this problem is fewer clinches and more conversation; more getting to know one another as persons instead of emphasizing the enjoyment of each other as bodies.

Do you have "sex questions" no one has adequately answered? Have you decided "what's smart for you" when it comes to dating standards? How is your "sex-judgment"? What are your guidelines for sex behavior?

Get help on thinking through these questions by talking to someone whose judgment you respect and whom you can trust—your pastor, your youth director, your Sunday School teacher, one of your parents, etc. (You may feel that you can trust no one who is older—particularly if he or she is over 30—and you may just have to "take a chance" but the risk can be worth it. There are a lot of levelheaded Christians who are interested in helping young people, but they don't quite know how to make the contact, and you may have to make the first step.)

Another thing you can do is read. Get books on the subject of sex and morals and take the time to read them. This might mean missing a few TV shows and cutting down on your bull sessions or phone conversation time, but it will be worth it. For a list of useful books, see pages 233 and 234.

CHAPTER 8

Is it worth it to wait?

> *There was a young lady named Wilde*
> *Who kept herself quite undefiled*
> *By thinking of Jesus*
> *And social diseases*
> *And the fear of having a child.*

This sarcastic and sacrilegious little limerick is used by sexual revolutionists to make fun of traditional morality. To hear the new morality tell it, in the past, people stayed "moral" sexually because of the consequences, but now there is little danger of venereal disease or unwanted premarital pregnancy. The pill and the needle have taken care of this. Contraceptive measures are almost "foolproof" and the miracle of antibiotic drugs is supposedly an instant cure for venereal disease.

These sound like excellent arguments, but one or two questions remain. If these dangers are not real, why has the number of cases of venereal disease skyrocketed in America, especially among teen-agers? Five times as many people become infected with venereal disease today as they did ten years ago. In the United States, 13-19-year-olds account for 25 percent of all cases of VD reported. In the 12-19 age group, syphilis has increased 200 percent in the last six years.*

VD unconquered, the pill not fail-safe

And, as for the "foolproof" qualities in the pill and other contraceptives . . . something seems amiss here as well. If prevention of premarital pregnancy is practically a "sure thing," why are the homes for unwed mothers doing a brisk business in red-eyed women from teen-age on up, who didn't think it would "happen to them"?

Particularly among teen-agers, the fallacy still exists that antibiotics such as penicillin are an instant "cure" for VD. This just isn't true. Treatment is often a long and complicated process. When the victim delays treatment, he risks permanent crippling, sterility and impotency. And, even if the victim gets early treatment, he faces the grisly fact that some of the bacteria that cause venereal diseases—especially gonorrhea—have developed a high degree of resistance to antibiotics since World War II.**

*The Pill and Its Impact, National Observer Newsbook. Copyright 1967 by Dow-Jones and Co., Inc., p. 65.
**For example, in Los Angeles county (California) authorities estimated in mid-1968 that there were 37,000 infected females, many of whom were unaware that they were infected. This group constituted a continuing reservoir of gonorrhea in the county. Los Angeles Times, July 7, 1968.

As for the "power of the pill," it is correct to say that the pill is highly effective in preventing pregnancy. It is not, however, 100 percent effective. *No contraceptive is 100 percent effective.* In addition, many people fail to understand how to use contraceptives. Still others, especially younger girls in their teens, fail to use them because in the heat of the passionate moment they don't want to get so "official and technical about it."

There is a lot of talk about birth control devices and the "power of the pill." Modern science has reduced greatly the odds against unwanted pregnancy, but the odds are still there. Many girls are still losing when they play the game of premarital sex.

A million criminal abortions are no joke

Hugh Hefner boasts in his "Playboy Philosophy" that his magazine likes to take a "recreational view of sex." Playboy strives to make sex look like a grand and glorious good time, but the girls in the homes for unwed mothers aren't laughing. And the girls who undergo some 1,000,000 criminal abortions per year aren't laughing either. In fact, every year, hundreds of girls and women come out of an abortion dead. Some try self-induced abortion methods that are extremely dangerous, such as using a knitting needle or a bent piece of wire. Others go to people who are "in the abortion business." Some of these abortionists are capable medical doctors, but others have little or no medical training.

Playboy's answer to the dangers of illegal abortion is to make abortion legal—especially in the United States. Abortion is legal in some foreign countries such as Sweden (and in some states in America*). According to Hugh Hefner and other advocates of the new morality such as Bishop John Robinson and Joseph Fletcher a great deal of heartache, misery and death could be avoided if girls could go openly to a hospital and have an abortion when they face an unwanted pregnancy.

"Playboy" battles "inadequate abortion laws"

Hefner carries on a running battle with the "inadequate abortion laws" that he finds on the law books throughout the United States. The "Playboy Forum," a monthly feature in *Playboy* magazine, contains dialogue between Hefner and other *Playboy* staff writers with readers on such topics as abortion, capital punishment, homosexuality and many other controversial subjects.

Playboy's position on abortion is that it is not homicide, and that if the woman does not want the baby, she should not have to bear it.

Just as with its charges against Puritanism, *Playboy's* arguments concerning abortion have an element of truth in them. Abortion laws in most states are antiquated and inadequate. The questions are many and there is sharp division over the issues. Is abortion always homicide? Can the human embryo be called a person, or is a fetus considered a person? When does an embryo or fetus receive a

*By 1968, California, Colorado and North Carolina had revised abortion laws so that abortion was legal if the mother's mental or physical health was threatened, if the pregnancy was the result of rape or incest and (in Colorado and North Carolina) if there was a chance that the baby might be born deformed.

soul? Is therapeutic abortion justifiable in order to save the mother's life? What about rape or incest? What about instances where a pregnant woman contracts German measles and faces a 30 percent chance that her child will be born blind or deformed?*

"Playboy" wants abortions to be legal because . . .

Playboy appears to be a noble champion of the downtrodden and abused as it mounts its white charger and humanely fights for the right of all women to have abortions if they want them. But with *Playboy's* basic approach to sex and morality, the very real question remains, "Is *Playboy* really doing nothing more than fighting for its point of view on premarital and extramarital sex?"

According to *Playboy's* point of view, you have the right to have all the sex where you want, when you want, with whom you want. It seems logical, then, that if you happen to slip up, it should be no great problem. You should be able to simply go down and have the "problem" extracted much as you would a bad tooth.

Playboy piously claims that women who face unwanted pregnancies need understanding and

*For an excellent discussion of abortion, see "Abortion: Is It Moral?" S. I. McMillen, M.D., *Christian Life*, September 1967, p. 32. A knowledgable Christian, Dr. McMillen goes into the problem of abortion with understanding and candor. At the same time, he does not back away from the moral issues involved. For example, he reports that of the 18,000 legal therapeutic abortions performed annually in this country, only 200 are due to rape or incest. He cautions that legalizing abortion for such causes as "emotional well-being" or "preservation of moral health" could open the way to rationalizing millions of additional criminal abortions. McMillen estimates that if one million criminal abortions are now being performed yearly, legalization of abortion could easily up the figure to 3 million. For further reading, see articles pertaining to abortion and contraception in *Christianity Today*, November 8, 1968.

compassion. This is certainly quite true. But it does not follow that one's "understanding and compassion" should reach the point where irresponsible use of sex is given carte blanche approval. For all of its tender talk about the poor girls who are victimized by unrealistic abortion laws, *Playboy* is really after a completely secular and humanistic society where everyone can have access to all of the scientific safeguards and remedies available while they "take their chances" with sex.

But what *Playboy* does not consider is the psychological and emotional consequences that misuse of sex can produce. Suppose wholesale abortions were legalized. Suppose some women and teen-age girls could have abortions with no regrets or guilt feelings. It simply does not follow that all women would find abortion to be the way out of a pregnancy problem.

The psychological effects of having an abortion are always present. The guilt and feelings of loss that remain after an abortion are caused by something far deeper than any "puritanical prudery" or the rules and codes of society. When a mother kills that which is living inside of her (and it *is* living whether an embryo or a fetus), she kills a little bit of herself. With many women, the scar will remain, no matter how "unwanted" the baby might have been.

For all of Hugh Hefner's talk about "responsible and mutually agreeable casual sex," *Playboy* magazine has yet to offer a good answer for the unmarried girl who becomes pregnant by her playboy. What if the girl will not be satisfied with either residency at a home for unwed mothers *or* an abortion—legal or illegal?

Playboy doesn't answer because it doesn't have an answer. The girl took her chances. She should have realized that it was all "just for kicks." She should have known that her playboy didn't really want any "permanent relationship." *Playboy's* "consolation" to the girl pregnant out of wedlock (and out of luck) is to run cartoons with punch lines that chuckle at her for being stupid enough to get "knocked up."

Playboy loves to preach Freudian psychology. It waggles a warning finger as it talks about all the dangers of "suppressed sex." To hear Hefner (and certain sociologists and psychologists with his point of view) tell it, remaining a virgin until marriage means running the "terrible risk of being frigid, impotent, or at best inexperienced."*

But what you don't read about in *Playboy* is the misery, the heartache, the ruined lives that come from premarital and extramarital affairs. Whenever two human beings come together in the most intimate act possible—sexual intercourse—there is more involved than physical appetite. People (especially women) can be hurt and hurt badly by "casual, recreational and uncommitted sex," be-

---

*"Playboy Philosophy," Installment 8, pp. 5-7. *Playboy's* Freudianism is actually "pseudo-psychology." It throws around terms like suppression of sex (actually the more accurate term is repression) and tries to convince its readers that attempts at sexual "self-control" are psychologically harmful. As Rev. Canon Bryan Green, who has lectured to thousands of co-educational university groups throughout the English speaking world, points out, in psychology, repression is not a conscious effort of self-control. Repression is to keep deep down in the subconscious an emotion that you do not want to face consciously. *Playboy's* pitch that self-control in regard to sex can lead to frigidity, impotency, etc., is a lot of bunk.

PLAYBOY PREACHES PSEUDO-PSYCHOLOGY

cause they are people—they are human beings with feelings, emotions, weaknesses and vulnerabilities of all kinds.

Not everyone can play *Playboy's* game of "eat, drink and have recreational sex unlimited." The files of psychiatrists and psychologists are packed with the same dreary plot. Boy meets girl. One or both have wide open attitudes toward morality, so they do what comes naturally with "no regrets." But later (often sooner) the relationship sours. The playboy moves on (or the girl wakes up to the fact that he "really isn't Mr. Dreamboat after all").

Even if there is no pregnancy or VD, there is always having to live with yourself. There is always the danger of coming out of such a relationship with a shattered or a badly bruised psyche. There is always having to remember that you gave yourself to someone else who used you and then discarded you with the same ease that a monkey discards a banana peel.

The case of Cynthia, girl friend No. 3

In the last few years *Playboy* has changed its tune a bit and now indignantly protests when anybody writes in accusing them of making girls into objects to be displayed on the playboy's arm. No, no, the prudes have us all wrong, says the "Playboy Forum." The monthly Playmate is not a depersonalized, dehumanized object. In addition to the 3-page fold out of the Playmate in all her natural beauty, there are many other pages showing her dating her boyfriend, strolling along the beach, even sitting on the couch with dear old dad. Playmates have names, addresses, ideas, attitudes, ambitions, hopes and fears. How can anyone say that the Playmate is "dehumanized and depersonalized"?

The answer is simple. You don't have to take away a girl's name to depersonalize her. For proof you can trace the history of a four-time *Playboy* cover girl who was "fortunate enough" to be chosen as Hugh Hefner's "special" girl friend.

Cynthia Maddox came to work at *Playboy* as a typist right out of high school in 1959. She soon became Hefner's third "special girl"* which means that she lived in cohabitation with him in the erotic, exciting, extravagant surroundings of the Playboy Mansion on Chicago's north side.

At first, life as Bunny No. 1 was exciting and oh, so romantic. But it wasn't long until disillusionment began to set in. Cynthia Maddox found that after all of the "glamour and romance" she was still left with

*Preceding Cynthia were Betty and Joyce. See "Hugh Hefner: 'I Am in the Center of the World'," Oriana Fallaci, *Look*, January 10, 1967, p. 57.

a "human being"—who soon began his usual pattern of "extra-curricular activity."

Not that Hefner was a hypocrite. He definitely played it straight with Cynthia just as he does with all his special girl friends. He did not go out on her behind her back. In fact, he let her watch.

Cynthia tried to maintain the "who cares" attitude, but inside it was "killing her." Cynthia got so frustrated by the "glories of cohabitation" with Hugh Hefner that she had temper tantrums. She ran around his office trampling layout, scattering copy, etc.; and this proved to be a "great outlet" for her. (Who would think that "unsuppressed sex" would end up like *this?*)

Inevitably, Cynthia got traded in

Eventually and inevitably, of course, Cynthia got "traded in" for a new model. She still had her name and she was definitely a "personality" but—she wasn't quite sure who she was. She told a *Life* magazine reporter that sometimes she didn't feel like she had any identity of her own.

After being dropped by Hefner, she was known as Hugh's old girl friend, a *Playboy* cover girl, and therefore "fair game," a trophy that a lot of men would like to hang on their bedroom wall. They regarded her as the living and breathing embodiment of everything *Playboy* stands for, and they treated her accordingly.

What was Hugh Hefner's comment? He is quoted in the same *Life* article as saying that he picks good looking young girls because he gets something very good out of the innocence and sweetness in them. He proudly points out that most of the girls he has gone out with have benefited from the experience because he gives them an identity and when they come out of the "machine" they are better for it.*

And so, Hefner moved on to another "special girl"—Mary Warren, 19, who was also featured in the *Life* magazine article that told about Cynthia. Mary enjoyed the pleasures of the mansion for two years, then moved out. "I date others," explained Hefner, "which to her is a source of pain."

Despite the obvious emptiness in his "I'll use you, then you'll use me" treatment of women, Hefner has spared no wrath or scorn on anyone who prefers the Biblical approach to morality. One of his favorite targets is Ann Landers, well-known advisor to the love-, and sex-lorn in a syndicated column published in many newspapers throughout the country.

In Installment VIII of the "Playboy Philosophy" Hefner attacks the practical suggestions in Miss Landers' booklet, *Necking, Petting, and How Far to Go.* He says that her admonitions against heavy necking and petting are what produce generations of frigid, impotent and sexually maladjusted people.** Hefner's authority for his rebuttal to Miss

*Shades of Joseph Fletcher and his co-hero of *Situation Ethics*—The Rainmaker—noble hero of the hayloft who fornicated with the rancher's daughter in order to give her a sense of womanliness (see Chapter 3). For the complete story of Cynthia Maddox and other special girl friends, see "In Hefnerland, Women Are Status Symbols," Diana Lurie, *Life*, October 29, 1965, pp. 70, 71 and also p. 68.
**Here we are, back to Hefner's pseudo-psychology again. He is trying to make Ann Landers' advice to develop self-control sound like "repression," which is not (see footnote, p. 142). Ann Landers has spoken and written to millions of teen-agers with a "straight from the shoulder" approach to sex that leaves them saying "She knows the score" . . . "We're not kidding her" . . . "She's got us pegged." See "Ann Landers," Part II, Pete Martin, *Christian Life*, June, 1966, p. 22.

PLAYBOY GIVES ANN LANDERS "BAD PRESS"

Landers is (you guessed it) Dr. Kinsey. The gist of Kinsey's argument (and that makes it Hugh Hefner's argument) is that "everybody pets, so why fight it?"

This is, of course, the familiar bandwagon argument that was discussed in Chapter 7. The bandwagon argument has many weaknesses, but it also is very potent—especially if you are young and unmarried. The sex drive that God has put in all of us is a powerful force, and it is even powerful enough to overcome arguments against premarital sex that are based on the dangers of unwanted pregnancy, venereal disease, or the emotional price that you might have to pay. Unfortunately, the power of sex can even overcome the excellent advice that Ann Landers has given to today's youth: "Be good because it's smart."

"It's smart to be good," but . . .

Many a young man and young woman is well aware that "it's smart to be good," but being smart can also be a drag. Human beings are made to feel, to experience, to enjoy. God made each one of us with a wide range of emotions. We can laugh, we can cry, we can shout with glee and mope around in depression. Feelings are part of being human. Feelings are part of having a human spirit.

Hugh Hefner capitalizes on the fact that man has feelings. His philosophy says: "You have hungers and desires, so why not satisfy them? These are God-given, so why deny yourself?"

What's the answer? The answer lies in that same human spirit that responds to the gamut of emotions and feelings. "Being smart" is never the ultimate motive for the Christian to "be good." The Christian who knows what the Bible teaches (not what Hugh Hefner thinks it teaches*) realizes that he not only has the image of God within him, but he has God Himself in the person of the Holy Spirit. This is why Paul concludes his argument against fornication in I Corinthians 6 by saying:

"That is why I say to run from sex sin (fornication). No other sin affects the body as this one does. When you sin this sin it is against your own body. Haven't you

---

*For example, Hefner thinks that Christ's teaching on the meek inheriting the earth (Matt. 5:5) was fine for a time when nearly all men were slaves, but the free men in a democracy have a right to be heard, to compete, to rebel and bring progress ("Playboy Philosophy" Installment II, p. 8; Installment VIII, p. 4). Apparently, Hefner has never bothered to consider the meaning of "meek" in this passage: "Unselfish, possessor of a courageous, calm humility." Jesus was "meek;" but He also drove the money changers out of the temple. And, if there was ever anyone who rebelled against the establishment and brought progress to the world, it was Jesus Christ.

146

yet learned that your body is the home of the Holy Spirit God gave you, and that He lives within you? Your own body does not belong to you. For God has bought you with a great price. So use every part of your body to give glory back to God, because He owns it" (I Cor. 6:18-20, *Living New Testament*).

The ultimate argument for morality

Here, in capsule form, is the ultimate argument from Scripture for forsaking fornication and adultery. Here is the Christian's authority for telling Hugh Hefner (or any other playboy or playmate): "No thanks, your package of pleasure looks attractive, but I have a 'hang-up' you can't understand. You see, I'm committed to a Person. This Person possesses me, and yet, it's a funny thing. He doesn't dominate me. Jesus Christ doesn't use me for His own ends and He still gives me pleasure, joy and self-fulfillment that I couldn't possibly find any other way."

This isn't always an easy speech to make. And, let's face it . . . there are a lot of church members who don't feel that they can honestly say this. There are a lot of church members who fall for *Playboy's* anti-Christ, anti-Bible, hedonistic philosophy. Some of these church people are clergymen who write letters to the "Playboy Forum" castigating the pharisaism and legalism of the church and cheering *Playboy* on because it is so honest, so humane, and so "like Jesus."

This is an ironic victory for *Playboy* to win, but it is no victory over Jesus Christ or Scripture. It is a victory over the person who has confused Chris-

PLAYBOY'S PHILOSOPHY (CONDENSED)

tianity with religion and who fails to recognize that *Playboy* is:

(1) *hedonistic humanism* that glorifies man as basically good and perfectible.

(2) *rationalistic, agnostic naturalism* that is utterly opposed to supernaturalism.

(3) *a secular point of view* that seeks to fulfill the physical desires of the moment and which has little regard for future consequences and absolutely no sense of responsibility to Almighty God.

Hefner sounds convincing to the church member who has a faith that is basically allegiance to a certain code, but Christianity is not allegiance to codes. Christianity is not a religion that includes "quaint pastimes" like praying, singing hymns, and taking communion. These are all practices that Christians do, but behind all of these practices should be the motive and the power that can only

148

be generated by a personal relationship to Jesus Christ.

Real Christianity is no cliché

The idea of a "personal relationship to Christ" is not easy to describe. In fact, the phrase can easily become a cliché, but the Bible makes it plain that what Christ did for the world is no cliché. The Bible makes it plain that when a person repents of (turns from) his sin and believes in Christ, something happens. He is born again. He becomes a new person. He turns from one way of living and one set of values (essentially the kind of values worshipped by *Playboy*) to a completely new outlook and way of being. The Christian's body becomes the home of the Holy Spirit Himself. The Christian's body is not his own; it is God's. God bought it with a great price—the shed blood of Jesus Christ.*

The Christian who correctly understands salvation from sin sees it as far more than "fire insurance" that assures him of arrival in heaven. The Christian who receives Christ not only receives the gift of salvation, but also assumes the responsibility to give glory back to God.** An important part of giving glory back to God is how the Christian uses his body, how he obeys God's commandments.

A lot of what passes for Christianity is nothing more than mental assent to the "moral teachings of Christ." But a "philosophy" called "Christian love" is no match for *Playboy's* hedonistic humanism.

The whole question boils down to the same issue

*See John 3:1-8; II Cor. 5:17; Rom. 8:1-11; I Peter 2:24; I Cor. 6:19,20.
**See Eph. 2:8-10; I Cor. 10:31; John 14:21.

that has divided Biblical Christianity from mere religion or secular philosophy ever since that third morning after the crucifixion. Either Christ died for our sins and rose again on the third day from the dead according to the Scripture or He didn't. Either God entered this world in the human form of Jesus Christ or He didn't. Either man is a sinner or he isn't. Either Christianity is a supernatural faith that explains the questions that naturalism can't answer or it isn't. Either God's reasons for "fleeing fornication" and not committing adultery are sound and authoritative or they aren't.

It's worth it to wait IF . . .

Is it worth it to wait? Is it worth it to suffer the pains and frustration of chastity in favor of using sex as God planned it instead of letting yourself go as *Playboy* urges? Is it worth it to try to master your habits, desires, and appetites instead of becoming a slave to them?

It all depends. It all depends on a very key choice: *what will you do with Jesus Christ?* Not the caricature of Christianity that is drawn by *Playboy* magazine . . . not the religious philosophies of liberal theologians who call themselves Christians. What will you do with Jesus Christ? God Himself, who has made claims on your life that you cannot ignore.

That bit of sarcastic rhyme about the young lady named Wilde, does, after all, give you solid reasons for waiting. VD and pregnancy out of wedlock are still valid reasons to "be good," because it *is* smart not only for the individual, but for all society. But the ultimate reason for Christians to stay undefiled by the misuse of sex is because of Jesus' love for them and their love for Jesus. Love goes where the law can't—into your soul—where decisions about right and wrong are really made.

It boils down to simple but profound choices—choices that determine the course of your entire life.

Religious rules and regulations ... or a personal relationship to Christ.

Seeking pleasure for yourself . . . or finding self-fulfillment in knowing God.

It all depends . . .

TAKE TIME ...

Use the following ideas to take time to apply the Bible to your life and any situations you face.

The final case against fornication

[18]"That is why I say to run from sex sin. No other sin affects the body as this one does. When you sin this sin it is against your own body. [19]Haven't you yet learned that your body is the home of the Holy Spirit God gave you, and that He lives within you? Your own body does not belong to you. [20]For God has bought you with a great price. So use every part of your body to give glory back to God, because He owns it" (I Cor. 6:18-20, *Living New Testament*).

Write in your own words why it's worth it to wait until marriage to have sex.

Is it really worth it to you? Or is the price just a little higher than you want to pay? You will have to weigh that yourself: the price God paid for you against the price you have to pay to bring glory back to Him. As C. S. Lewis said, there is no more unpopular Christian virtue than chastity, but perhaps that is what makes it a virtue. It all depends . . .

TAKE INVENTORY . . .

In his book, *The Stork Is Dead*, Charlie Shedd presents a list of "lines guys use" on girls to get them to go farther than they want to. The list is for "girls only," but fellows might read it too just to see if this is the kind of chatter they are handing out in order to see how far they can get.

The wounded pigeon. His line is "The world is so unfair. See how they pick on me. Nobody treats me right but you." (Be careful, this brings out a girl's mothering instinct and she can easily wind up a mother.)

The "poor little you" line. Opposite of the wounded pigeon: "You have never been loved right. Your folks, brothers, sisters, grandmother, teachers, stepmother, the whole world—they've given you such a bad deal. I'm so sorry. Poor little unloved you." (Watch it—especially if you start hearing yourself saying: "He understands me perfectly.")

The "prove your love or go away" line. As old as Adam, undoubtedly a favorite of prehistoric petting enthusiasts. (A very effective weapon on the girl who feels "It would just kill me if I lost him!")

The "everybody does it" line. "What's the matter with you, anyway? You come over with the Puritans or something? Join the party! Live a little!" (A *Playboy* favorite. Especially potent when used on girls who have been going stir crazy sitting at home waiting for dates.)

The "let me make a woman out of you" line. Variations: "I'm about to complete your life, right now, darling." . . . "Let me be your teacher!" (Can't you hear The Rainmaker telling the rancher's daughter this one up in the hayloft? See Chapter 3.)

The "men want experienced women" line. "All the fellows these days prefer girls who know how to do it." (Until they decide to find one for marriage. Then, all of a sudden, they decide that "no experience is really necessary.")

The "we're going to get married anyway" line. "What's a little slip of paper between people like us? We'll make it legal sometime anyway." (Nicely countered by: "But, Jimmy, I love you so much and I wouldn't want you ever to feel obligated to me.")

The "anything we do is OK so long as we don't go all the way" line. (As Charlie Shedd comments, the fellow who uses this line usually has a "great pair of hands . . . expert in the erogenous zones.") But petting is not OK because: (a) some feelings are for marriage alone; (b) you might get so stirred you might lose your head and your virginity; (c) premarital intercourse isn't the only sin; (d) some habits developed now will hamper you later.")*

TAKE ACTION . . .

One of the books that you should be sure to read is:
Why Wait Till Marriage, Evelyn Millis Duvall. Association Press, 1965—an excellent book that tells it like it is concerning the pitfalls in premarital sex and the reasons why a self-controlled sex drive is worth every "pain racked, inhibiting moment."

If you are dating steadily and the question of "Why should we wait any longer?" is no longer an academic one, answer the following questions for yourself, and then if possible talk them over with the fellow or girl in question:

Questions for Him

Do you believe you really love the girl, or does biological pressure make the question a rather fuzzy one? Suppose you believe that you really do love her. Are you willing to put her in any position where you could cause great damage to her reputation, possibly her body, and most certainly her soul and emotions? To put it another way, if you really love her, can you risk hurting her terribly?

Do you feel that you are ready to take on the responsibility of marriage? Sex is one of the privileges of marriage. Do you believe that you have a right to the privileges of marriage without being ready or willing to take on the responsibilities?

Suppose just the sight of this gal puts your sex drive in

*Adapted from *The Stork Is Dead,* Charlie Shedd. Copyright 1968, Word Books, Waco, Texas.

153

overdrive. Do you believe that you are absolutely at the mercy of your physical appetites? To put it another way, do you feel that you are absolutely a slave to natural desire? Is there nothing you can do to "lower the temperature" in your relationship? If you're doing a lot of heavy necking and petting, up to, but just short of intercourse, is the pleasure worth the frustration? The inevitable result of heavy petting will be going all the way. And even if you somehow remain technically virgin, this hardly excuses you from the charge of fornication. If Christ can equate a lustful look with adultery, there seems to be little doubt that heavy petting is to be equated with fornication. Paul says to flee from sex sin (fornication). Are you willing to do this, or are you determined to follow a present path because deep inside you really want to "score" or "prove that you're a man."

In regard to "keeping things cool" have you prayed about this alone? Together with her? This idea would make any playboy or holder of secular values and views on sex laugh out loud or at least smile with disdain. For the Christian, however, praying is the most powerful weapon he has. Prayer is the button that turns on the power of Christ and the Holy Spirit in your life. Push that button *hard* and often.

Questions for Her

Do you believe you really love the guy, or do your emotions and your need to be wanted make the question a rather fuzzy one? Suppose you are convinced that you really do love him? Are you willing to put yourself in a position where you could suffer great harm mentally, physically, emotionally and spiritually? Also, are you willing to put him in a position where he can suffer—probably not physically—but certainly mentally, emotionally and spiritually? (Of course, he may be telling you he is "suffering" right now because of being sexually stimulated, but is this kind of suffering caused by guilt or other harmful and destructive conditions? Always keep in mind that "suppression of sex" is not harmful to the couple that is weighing all the factors in a relationship of real love.)

Do you feel you are ready to take on the responsibilities of marriage? Are you ready to care for a husband, a home, and possibly children?

Sex is one of the privileges of marriage. Do you believe that you have the right to the privileges of marriage without being willing to take on the responsibilities?

A girl's first sexual experience is very important to her. If you are a virgin, does the prospect of having intercourse outside of marriage seem worth it? Will you engage in it with no feeling of guilt, with relaxed security that will help you draw closer to the one you love? To put it another way, just what is sex to you? A "natural drive" that should be satisfied? Or does it have a much deeper psychological and emotional meaning?

A lot of couples think that they can "pet a little bit" and it won't hurt anything. After all, the Kinsey report says everybody is doing it. But does petting really help, or does it make things worse? As a couple pets, they usually find that they "begin where they left off" each time they do it.

As one of the "under 25 generation" has put it: "Making out is like a toboggan slide. Once you get on it, you have to keep on going, and somewhere before the bottom there is likely to be a crack-up."* Are you risking getting on that toboggan slide in order to be sure that "he loves you" or that you can somehow keep him through permitting intercourse? Is this the kind of relationship you really want with someone you believe you love?

Have you faced up to this problem openly and honestly with him? Have you done anything to try to "cool things down"? Have the two of you sought counsel from someone you feel you can trust?

If you are a Christian, "have you prayed about it?" This is a cliché only if that is what prayer is in your life. "Praying about it" is the most potent weapon a Christian has if he can really talk to God honestly, openly, sincerely. Prayer is the key to walking after the Holy Spirit and letting the Holy Spirit bear his fruit in your life. Keep in mind that one of those fruits is self-control (Gal. 5:23) and a little more self-control never hurt anyone.

The questions above are admittedly for people at a certain point in an interpersonal relationship. It may be that for you these questions are all "passe" or they are premature.

If these questions are passe—meaning that you have already "gone all the way" then remember that in God's score book, one error or even several errors does not put you out of the ball game. If you sincerely feel sorry

*"Danger, Marriage Ahead," Bruce Shelley, *United Evangelical Action*, June, 1966, p. 6.

about and reject what you have been doing (the Biblical term is repent) and you want to stop it, God will forgive you and you can start all over in His sight. God is a loving God and He can redeem any of us from mistakes that we make.

All of these questions are premature for you if you aren't dating or if you are simply "playing the field" without a lot of emotional involvements. But go through these questions anyway. Think through exactly how you would answer them if you ever would face this situation. There is a very good possibility that you will face the situation in which you will become very fond of a member of the opposite sex. How will you act—and why?

CHAPTER 9

One plus one equals one

To hear *Playboy* tell it, Christianity has a masochistic* point of view on life, teaching that sex is inherently sinful and is only to be tolerated because there is no other means to reproduce the human race. Hugh Hefner claims that the teachings about the "evils of sex" did not come from Christ, but were derived mainly from the writings of the apostle Paul, whose letters to the various churches make up much of the New Testament.

According to Installment 10 of Hefner's "Playboy Philosophy," Paul was definitely antisexual, and it was because of Paul's writings—particularly from I Corinthians 7—that the church developed a puritanical and antisexual viewpoint.

Hefner "correctly" quotes a phrase from I Cor. 7:1: "It is good for a man not to touch a woman ..." but then the fighter for free enterprise and fairplay

---

*A masochist is one who enjoys pain and abuse; his opposite is a sadist, who gets extreme pleasure from dishing out pain and abuse.

with all individuals goes on to tack on some segments from a completely different letter that Paul wrote to the church at Rome—Rom. 7:18,19 and 24, a classic passage in which Paul plumbs profoundly the depths of sinful man's experience.

When Hefner gets through with this bit of "editing" Paul looks like he has said this about sex: "It is good for a man not to touch a woman ..." and further, "For I know that in me dwelleth no good thing . . . for the good that I would do, I do not; but the evil which I would not, that I do. . . . Oh wretched man that I am! Who shall deliver me from the body of this death?"*

Biblical interpretation—"Playboy" style

Hefner does not bother to give the Biblical references for what he is quoting. He simply strings these two quotations together in order to "prove" that Paul had an extremely guilt-ridden and pessimistic view of both man and sex. The net result, of course, is that anyone reading Hefner's philosophy who has not bothered to check Scripture and read what Paul really did write about sex could easily conclude that the Bible is against sex and Christians who believe the Bible have "sexual hang-ups."

The truth of the matter—as the reading of I Corinthians 7 and other parts of Scripture will bring out—is that instead of being antisexual with some perverted, ascetic kind of self-denial, *Paul was actually warning the Corinthian Christians against this very attitude.* He was answering a question that they had put to him in a previous letter—a

*See "Playboy Philosophy," Installment 10, p. 1.

question that apparently was worded something like this: "Since there is so much sexual immorality around us, don't you think the best thing to do is to not engage in sexual intercourse under any circumstances, not even within marriage?"

But because Paul's answer to the question included the phrase about not "touching a woman" he has been labeled "antisexual" by various liberal scholars* down through the centuries. It is quite possible to take Paul's words here and interpret them in a way that concludes Paul was antisexual. It is also quite possible to look into the context of the passage and to get at what Paul was really saying.

What Paul was saying here is, "Your idea of a man not touching a woman is a bit idealistic and unrealistic. Men and women just aren't made that way and it would be far better for you to go ahead and get married in order to avoid frustration and immorality."

It is also difficult to find "antisexualism" in Paul's clear teaching in the next few verses—I Cor. 7:3-5. Paul clearly says that husbands and wives should give each other their "conjugal rights" meaning in plain English, sex. He also says that they should never use sex as some sort of weapon or tool of blackmail to punish one another. They should love each other enough to give their bodies to one another because each is the rightful possessor of the other's body.

*Hefner gets virtually all of his ideas on Christianity and religion from liberals. For example, when writing about Paul's "antisexuality" he quotes from John Short in the *Interpreter's Bible,* a liberal commentary on Scripture.

It's obvious, of course, that Paul and a lot of those early Christians were all hung up with antisexual attitudes.

In his "Playboy Philosophy," Hugh Hefner points to the errors of the early Christian church in regard to sex. Hefner tries to get his readers to swallow reasoning that goes something like this: "Some of those early Christians like Origin castrated themselves because they were so hung-up with Paul's antisexual teachings. Because these early Christians had such twisted ideas, it follows that Christianity is all wrong, the Bible is all wet, and Playboy is all right." But nowhere in Scripture is there any guarantee that believers in Christ instantaneously became infallible. Because some of the early Christians sincerely but mistakenly over-reacted against the incredible pagan immorality around them is hardly proof that Playboy's exploitation of sex for profit is right. Hefner's disdain for "religion" is obvious, but he is rebelling against his strict, puritanical upbringing, not what the Bible really teaches about sex.

When Paul tried to straighten out the Corinthian Christians and get them to abandon (not adopt) a puritanical view of sex, he was merely substantiating the overall Biblical teaching that sex in marriage is good and wonderful. Because he had been reared in the finest of Hebrew tradition, Paul knew well the Lord's positive commandment to man to "be fruitful and multiply" (Gen. 1:28). No Jewish man of Paul's day would have foregone marriage except possibly for a lifetime of study in the law. To the Jew, marriage and having children was a commandment that was not to be denied.

According to Old Testament Scripture, marriage is an institution planned by God from the very beginning—in fact, before the fall. One of the

Bible's key passages on sex and marriage is found in Gen. 2:18-24. Human sexuality is actually the result of God's fatherly concern for mankind. That is why He said: "It is not good that the man should be alone. I will make a helper fit for him." Like everything else that God created, human sexuality is right and good. Through selfishness, pride and lust, man may twist his sexuality, but this is not as God planned it nor as God wants it.*

Prudes or playboys—both miss the point

Sex should never be seen by man as a "necessary evil to reproduce the race," nor should it be viewed as the "be-all and end-all" of life. The "necessary evil" point of view is that taken by the prude, the pietistic Puritan who has the idea that there is something "dirty" about sex. The "be-all and end-all" extreme is the one that is taken by *Playboy*, because *Playboy* emphasizes the physical side, the satisfaction of physical need and desire.

The Biblical view sees sexual relationships as the self-surrender of two people to each other. One person surrenders his private identity to another private identity and they become a single corporate identity. In sexual intercourse, two persons really become one person. From the perspective of Scripture, sexual intercourse is synonomous with being married.**

According to God's arithmetic, the institution of marriage has an equation that reads: one plus one

---

*"Sex in a Theological Perspective," Donald Bastian. *Christianity Today*, July 19, 1968, p. 7.
**"Sex and the Silent Revolution," Duane Mahl, *This Day*, January, 1968.

equals one. Or, to put it in the way we often hear as people speak of marriage: "two become one." In marriage, we find the intertwining of the complete lives of two distinct personalities. That is why the Bible uses the term "one flesh." It is describing a relationship that is so profound and so enduring that only a term like "one flesh" can adequately do the job.*

Man corrupted God's gift of sex

Sex was one of God's most wonderful gifts to man, but like so many gifts, it was corrupted. When man fell, sex fell along with him and became one of man's many tools for rebellion against God. But through it all, the Bible still holds the highest view and praise for the correct use of sex in a relationship of love between a man and a woman.

The Scriptures contain many passages that would make the typical prude blush a Puritan pink. See, for example, the Song of Solomon, especially a passage like Chapter 7. Here is a frank description of erotic love that would do *Playboy* proud (and some good).

"Oh, how delightful you are; how pleasant, O love, for utter delight! You are tall and slim like a palm tree, and your breasts are like its clusters of dates. I said, I will climb up into the palm tree and take hold of its branches. Now may your breasts be like grape clusters, and the scent of your breath like apples, and your kisses as exciting as the best of wine, smooth and sweet . . ." (Song of Solomon 7:6-9, *Living Lessons of Life and Love*).

*"Sex in a Theological Perspective," Donald M. Bastian, *Christianity Today*, July 19, 1968, p. 7.

Marriage illustrates God's love for His own

Over and over again in the Bible, a relationship between a man and a woman, particularly a man and a wife, is used to illustrate God's love for His chosen people (Israel) and Christ's love for His church.*

It is worth noting that in the Bible's references to sex, sex is never an end but only a means—a means of engaging in the most intimate of interpersonal relationships. The sex act is probably the highest and most concentrated expression of love possible between two human beings. In the sex act, the individual can never come closer to losing himself in unity with another. And this is precisely why the Bible constantly uses the analogy of sexuality in marriage when it talks about the relationship between God and the believer. As one scholar points out, it is no accident that the church is referred to as the "bride of Christ."**

When God created sex, His purpose was to make possible a high and holy uniting of two personalities. Sex within marriage is the supreme earthly happiness that can be enjoyed by a man and a woman.

Because sex is so right within marriage is why God made it clear sex is so wrong outside marriage.

One writer puts it this way. "The Bible has a very dynamic idea about sex union: it does things to people; it doesn't leave them as they were before. 'For this

---

*For passages comparing God's love for his chosen people with the love of a man for his wife, see Isa. 51; Jer. 2 and 3; Hosea 1 and 3. For Paul's profound comparison of Christ's love for his church with the love shared by a man and his wife, see Eph. 5:22-25.

**"Love and Sexuality," Gary H. Gill, *Eternity*, September 1968, p. 11.

Why should we let something artificial, like a marriage ceremony, prevent us from being one?

THIS PHONY, PLAYBOY-TYPE QUESTION, HAS A VALID ANSWER

reason a man shall leave his father and mother and be joined to his wife and the two shall become one.' When a man and a woman become sex partners, something very strange happens. They become one flesh. They lose a certain amount of independence. Each one is an inseparable part of another's life. There is an invisible bond between them."*

Those who argue for premarital sex, especially "those who love each other" might reply, "all well and good. That's exactly what we want to do. We want to become one. We want to seal our relationship with an invisible bond. Why should something artificial like a marriage ceremony stand in our way?" A valid question, but it can be answered by equally valid questions: "If you truly intend to 'become one' with the one you say you love, why not be willing to wait until the time that you can publicly and openly—before God and all men—take each other as life partners in an act of com-

*The Two Shall Be One, Albert C. Winn. Copyright 1960, John Knox Press.

164

plete commitment? If sex is so important to you, why do you want to engage in it on a basis that is something less than final, complete and fully committed?"

Sex is not to be used selfishly. No matter how "desperate" the situation may seem for a young fellow and girl who plan to get married but can't at the moment—no matter how they long and yearn for each other—if they go ahead and go to bed together before entering into the commitment of marriage, they are using sex selfishly and sinfully. They are asking for trouble and trouble can come in many ways, as discussed in Chapters 7 and 8.

There is, of course, a possibility that the couple can "go ahead and get married anyhow." Many couples do just this. In fact, in the U. S. over half of all teen-age brides are pregnant at the altar. As well-known anthropologist Margaret Mead has observed, "Parents tell their children to be careful, but '... if you slip-up, we'll give you a nice church wedding.'" There is a sort of practical ethic among people today that says: "Well, as long as they get married and give the kid a name, what's the hurt?"

The "hurt" is that the couple who is expecting the baby at the altar has not only violated God's laws; this couple has marred the beginning of its marriage relationship with an act that is selfish and basically destructive to their relationship. Many marital troubles can be traced back to the fact that "she went all the way with me before we were married."*

*This is not to say that a couple who "have to get married" can't know God's forgiveness and grace as promised in I John 1:9. God, however, is just as well as forgiving. All of us—and perhaps married couples in particular—reap what we sow.

Experience is not necessary

Playboy claims that the more bed partners a man has before he enters marriage, the better husband he will make. By what strange twist of logic could becoming "one flesh" on a partial, perverted or promiscuous basis help a man gain deeper understanding of what it really means to give himself totally to a woman in complete love? Sleeping around might make you more sexually proficient (and then again, it might not). It might make you "more experienced" but it will not make you a better husband or wife.

Walter Trobisch worked for ten years in Africa and out of his experiences in counselling young African men and women, he wrote the book, *I Loved a Girl*. In Africa, to "love a girl" simply means to go to bed with her. It is a culture where there is little sexual restraint, no romance and no "in-between." A girl is simply a thing, an object. Trobisch believes that what Africa needs more than anything else is to learn how to love.

But he wonders if people in America and other western nations know much more about love than the Africans. He says:

"If Africa needs to learn how to love, America has to learn how to suffer. The sex problems in America may have their deepest roots in the refusal to accept suffering, in wanting to jump over the in-between stage with its tension and anxiety, and thus, however, to make the word 'love' as empty a word as it is in the African bush."*

*"Love Is a Feeling to Be Learned," Walter A. Trobisch, *His*, January, 1968, p. 7.

Trobisch writes of a girl named Evelyn who is on her way to meet her future husband, and as she rides along in the train she thinks about exactly how they came together and how Carl had won her to himself.

One thing Evelyn realized was that she had learned to love Carl, and she had not learned it through premarital sex. She also realized that premarital sex would never have given her the certainty she now had concerning her love for him. To have gone ahead and submitted to biological hunger would have meant missing the beauty of the in-between, the pain of waiting and the joy of suspense, the suffering that made them so happy. Evelyn knew that sex would have kept their love from a chance to grow. It would have meant picking the blossoms in April and therefore never harvesting the apples.

And then Trobisch switches the scene to Carl—to his stream of consciousness as he awaits Evelyn's arrival and thinks about how he had fallen in love with her. One thing that had attracted him to her above everything else was her virginity, which included an intriguing mixture of attractiveness and modesty. If she had been attractive without being modest she would have directed Carl into sexual adventure, perhaps, but they never would have gotten to marriage.

They had their temptations, but Evelyn had modestly refused his advances, and he was glad that she had. He had secretly hoped that she would resist, because her refusal to give him sex under cheap and unfulfilled conditions was greater proof of her

love than if she would have granted him that kind
of sex. Giving in to him would have hurt their love
and probably destroyed it.

Chastity—unpopular but worth it

C. S. Lewis, the famed Christian apologist, has
said: "Chastity is the most unpopular of the Christian virtues. There is no getting away from it; the
old Christian rule is: 'Either marriage with complete faithfulness to your partner or else total ab-
stinence.'"*

This is a hard saying. It is an unpopular saying.
It seems totally unreasonable to many a young couple that is "turned on" toward one another physically. And yet, it is the Biblical picture of sex. God has
painted this picture not because he has some sadis-
tic desire to tease and tantalize man with his own
sexuality. God wants the best for man, and that is
why the Bible teaches that sex is for the safety,
security and full commitment of the marriage relationship.

Walter Trobisch sums it up: "Love does not grow
out of sex, love must grow into sex."

TAKE TIME ...

Use the following ideas to take time to apply the
Bible to your life and any situations you face.

First Corinthians 7 is a controversial passage that has
caused a great deal of debate and misunderstanding on
Paul's view of sex and the marriage relationship.

In I Cor. 7:6-9, for example, it appears that Paul was
a life-long bachelor who may have been "against marriage."

*Mere Christianity, C. S. Lewis. Copyright 1952, The Macmillan Co., p.
89.

"I'm not saying you *must* marry; but you certainly *may* if you wish. ⁷I wish everyone could get along without marrying, just as I do. But we are not all the same. God gives some the gift of a husband or wife, and others He gives the gift of being able to stay happily unmarried. ⁸So I say to those who aren't married, and to widows—better to stay unmarried if you can, just as I am. ⁹But if you can't control yourselves, go ahead and marry. It is better to marry than to burn with lust" (I Cor. 7:6-9, *Living New Testament*).

Why does Paul talk about remaining single if possible? For the answer, you have to go to I Cor. 7:26-29 and 35-38:

²⁶"Here is the problem: we Christians are facing great dangers to our lives at present. In times like these I think it is best for a person to remain unmarried. ²⁷Cf course, if you already are married, don't separate because of this. But if you aren't, don't rush into it at this time. ²⁸But if you men decide to go ahead anyway and get married now, it is all right; and if a girl gets married in times like these, it is no sin. However, marriage will bring extra problems that I wich you didn't have to face right now. ²⁹The important thing to remember is that our remaining time is very short, [and so are our opportunities for doing the Lord's work]. For that reason those who have wives should stay as free as possible for the Lord;

³⁵"I am saying this to help you, not to try to keep you from marrying. I want you to do whatever will help you serve the Lord best, with as few other things as possible to distract your attention from Him. ³⁶But if anyone feels he ought to marry because he has trouble controlling his passions, it is all right, it is not a sin; let him marry. ³⁷But if a man has the willpower not to marry and decides that he doesn't need to and won't, he has made a wise decision. ³⁸So the person who

marries does well, and the person who doesn't marry does even better" *(Living New Testament).*

Is Paul "anti-marriage" in this passage, or is he mainly concerned about the troublesome times?

What is Paul's major concern? That everyone get married and "live happily ever after" or that all Christians serve Christ as best they can?

For additional teachings on marriage, see Gen. 2:24; Prov. 18:22; I Thess. 4:4; I Tim. 5:14; Eph. 5:22-33; Heb. 13:4.

TAKE INVENTORY . . .

Have you ever evaluated yourself along the lines of "Am I really ready for marriage?" or "Am I becoming the kind of person who is mature enough to get married some day?" Following are some questions asked by Charlie Shedd, author of *The Stork Is Dead.* Answer these questions quietly and honestly:

Do I want to let myself go? Am I ready to open the doors way down in my heart? Do I understand that the key to healthy marriage is full communication? How honest am I willing to be at sharing what's inside me? Are the two of us a good combination here?

Can I give words to my love freely? Is it easy for me to express appreciation? If it isn't, will I give it my best effort and keep trying? Am I tender enough to meet the needs of this person I might marry? Do I want to know what blocks the flow of my affection?

When there are differences between me and others, what do I do? Can I look inside myself to see where I might be wrong? Do I surface my hostilities by blaming others, or can I bring them out in a healthy way? Have I learned the mature way to say, "I don't like that" . . . "I do not agree" . . . "Let's discuss it."

Are my ideas of success healthy? Am I ambitious enough or over-ambitious? Would I drive too hard, or am I lazy? Is there a tendency to perfectionism in me and if so, do I know why? Does money mean more than it should mean? Am I willing to adjust my goals to another person's goals so that we will both be better people?

Shedd writes that if you are overwhelmed by these questions, he's glad. The kind of relationship that he is talking about—marriage—is every bit as big as that barrage of questions.

To be awed at how great love is; to be fully aware of what you aren't; this, says Shedd, is one of the first requirements for mature marriage.*

TAKE ACTION . . .

Do some additional reading on preparation for marriage and the kind of marriage partner that would be right for you. The following books can be obtained in practically any public library:

Letters to Karen, Charles W. Shedd. Copyright 1965, Abingdon Press.

Letters to Phillip: On How to Treat a Woman, Charles W. Shedd. Copyright 1968, Doubleday and Co., Inc.

Toward Christian Marriage, W. Melville Capper and H. Morgan Williams. Copyright 1958, Inter-Varsity Press.

Dear Abby on Marriage, Abigail Van Buren. Copyright 1962, McGraw-Hill Book Co.

Design for Christian Marriage, Dwight H. Small. Copyright 1959, Fleming H. Revell Co.

One writer has taken the trouble to figure that if a marriage lasted for fifty years, that means 26,297,280 minutes together.** Since marriage is supposed to be

---

The Stork Is Dead, Charlie W. Shedd. Copyright 1968, Word Books, Waco, Texas.
**"Rendezvous," Gary Dausey, *Campus Life*, February 1967, p. 36.

for keeps—for over 26 million minutes if necessary—it stands to reason that you ought to think through carefully what kind of a person you ought to marry.

How do you evaluate those whom you are dating? Is "a good time" your chief concern, or do you ever think about the question: "Is this the kind of person I would like to marry?"

Look over the following list and check off what you feel are the most important items to consider when thinking about a marriage partner. Then try rating some of your dates to see how they score.

Physical attraction—while sex isn't everything, 26 million minutes *is* a long time.

Mentally stimulating—a couple has to have more to talk about than nothing. 'Nuff said.

Ability to share life—to discuss, to be flexible, to enjoy living.

Concern and consideration. Often overlooked in the rush of romance, but inconsiderate mates ruin a lot of marriages.

Spiritual compatibility—in other words, is it important to you that your partner be a Christian?

CHAPTER 10

What if it doesn't work out?

Hank and Elaine got married in their late teens and Elaine went to work to help Hank get through college.

Hank was the "go-getter." In addition to his schooling, he played varsity basketball and also starred in the church softball and bowling teams. He taught a junior high Sunday school class and ran junior Christian Endeavor.

There was only one "thorn in Hank's flesh." His little bride kept bugging him about the fact that he only spent one evening or so per week at home.

The fact of the matter was that it was getting so bad that Elaine almost had to "make an appointment" with Hank to get to see him (unless she would be content with watching him perform at the softball diamond). Times when they could really talk together alone became rare and when they did occur, conversation dribbled off into nothing because they really didn't have much to talk about. Elaine tried to tell Hank how she felt but he would brush it aside and go on to tell her about a "great play" he had made in a recent ball game or he would begin listing all the things he had to do.

So, Elaine clammed up and went into "psychological seclusion," which in plain language means "slow burn."

Hank thought he had Elaine tamed until . . .

Hank thought he had her tamed and went on daily with his busy routine. But, one night he came rushing home to grab a bite of dinner before dashing off to the softball game. Only there wasn't any dinner. There wasn't any Elaine.

Grumbling about the fact that his wife "knew he had to play ball tonight and why did she have to be late?" Hank rustled some supper and dashed for the diamond. He returned home about ten o'clock and still no Elaine.

Hank finally phoned Elaine's mother and, happily, Elaine answered. Hank was relieved, but his first comment was, "Why didn't you have my dinner ready? You knew I had to eat and run tonight."

This was the last straw for Elaine. She had decided to go straight to her mother's after finishing work because she was tired of living with a "boarder" who didn't pay much attention to her. She had to "get a message" to Hank somehow, and perhaps not showing up to fix his dinner would do the trick.

But when Hank finally phoned her and greeted

her with a complaint about his dinner and having to eat and run that night, Elaine slammed down the phone. Her "slow burn" turned into "cold storage." It took a lot of pleading by crestfallen Hank, plus no small amount of persuasion from in-laws and the pastor before Elaine would even consent to talk to her husband again and discuss their problems.*

This turbulent kind of tale has been, and is being, repeated in many marriages. While Hank and Elaine were able to patch things up, many, far too many, couples are not. The divorce rate in America is climbing with all the speed of an Apollo rocket. In 1967, 534,000 U. S. marriages were dissolved in the courts, a record. The number of children in families headed only by a woman had increased from 4,100,000 in 1953 to 7 million in 1966, the latest available figure.**

Cynical views on marriage are quite common. Some see it as a "stupid and hollow institution" in this enlightened day and age. The British Humanist Society has gone so far as to suggest that marriage be done away with completely.

Many marriages have a "reserve clause"

This cynical attack has undermined the institution of marriage. More and more young people are dubious about "making a go" of marriage. Many of them approach marriage with a "reserve clause" in mind: "Well, if it doesn't work out, we can always get a divorce."

*Adapted from an account in "Marriage Is for Adults Only," Laars I. Granberg, *Eternity,* January 1961, p. 7.
**"The Growing Toll of America's 'Broken Homes'," *U. S. News and World Report,* August 5, 1968, p. 92.

We'll try it, Lord, but if it doesn't work out, please bless our divorce.

CAN CHRISTIANS PUT AN ESCAPE CLAUSE IN MARRIAGE?

In the United States, one out of four marriages ends in divorce, and lots more marriages, while still intact, are in trouble to one degree or another. It is no wonder, then, that many people—especially those under 25—are asking if marriage is really worth it. And if they still think it really is worth it, they are not quite sure they can make it work.

And what about Christian marriage? Does knowing Christ as Saviour and Lord give you any guarantee that your marriage will be a roaring success? Can Christians enter into marriage with the "escape hatch" approach? Can they pray, "We'll try it, Lord, but if it doesn't work out, we hope you will bless our divorce?"

What does the Bible really say?

Paul, the apostle, wrote to the Christian church at Corinth with a "command from the Lord," that a husband and wife should not separate, and if they did, they should not remarry. (See I Cor. 7:10-11, *Living New Testament*.) Even in cases where one of the marriage partners became a Christian and the other remained in the grip of pagan idolatry, Paul's advice was for the Christian member to do his or her best to keep the marriage together.

Paul made it plain that Christians should, "Be sure in deciding these matters that you are living as God intended, marrying or not marrying in accordance with God's direction and help, and accepting whatever situation God has put you into" (I Cor. 7:17, *Living New Testament*). This was Paul's rule for all the churches as he echoed the clear teaching of Christ, which is found in Matt. 19:1-11.

Did Jesus permit divorce?

In Matthew 19, Jesus faced one of the many situations when the Pharisees tried to trip Him up with sticky questions. In this encounter they threw one of the stickiest of them all: " 'Do you permit divorce?' they asked" (Matt. 19:3, *Living New Testament*).

What made this such a sticky question was that there was a great deal of controversy among the Jews concerning divorce. Among the Pharisees—the religious and intellectual elite of the Jewish nation —there were two schools of thought on divorce: the Shammai and the Hillel. The Shammai said a man could give his wife a "bill of divorcement"* for unfaithfulness only—adultery or fornication. The

---

*See Deut. 24:1. The key phrase is "some uncleanness in her." The Shammai said this meant only adultery, the Hillel interpreted it to mean just about anything a man wanted to find wrong with his wife.

Hillel, however, said a man could divorce his wife for arguing too loudly with him, burning dinner, and even if he found a woman he thought more attractive.

In Matt. 19:5,6, Christ seems to agree with the Shammai. He says that a man is forever united to his wife to become one and no man should divorce what God has joined together. Later, in v. 9, He specifies that the only possible reason for divorce is fornication and adultery.

Why then, asked the Pharisees, did Moses write in Deut. 24:1 that a man could divorce his wife with a letter of dismissal (Matt. 19:7)? Jesus answered that Moses allowed this letter of dismissal in recognition of a hard fact of life—that men had hard and evil hearts and that the marriage relationship didn't always work. The point is that God's purpose —His will—was that marriage should not be broken. (See Matt. 19:8,9.)

There are two key points in what the Bible says about marriage and divorce.

God's will is that no marriage should be broken. There should be no divorce. (See Matt. 5:32; Mark 10:7,8; Rom. 7:2; I Cor. 7:10,11; Matt. 19:1-11.)

"He's a Zen Buddhist, but I love him so"

Christians should marry Christians. Paul recognized that marriage partners who are committed to Christ as well as to each other have a much greater chance of making marriage a success. That's why he cautions to marry only in the Lord (I Cor. 7:39). That's why he admonishes to "Be ye not unequally yoked together with unbelievers" (II Cor. 6:14).

178

Unfortunately, it seems that when the chips are down, many a Christian goes ahead and marries someone who possesses a completely different point of view. The Christian who marries an unbeliever is acting in direct disobedience to Christ and he or she is asking for trouble in the marriage relationship. This is the clear teaching of II Cor. 6:14; Eph. 5:6-10 and I John 1:6.

Any marriage is a risk

Let's be honest, marriage is a risk. The typical couple might not make the same mistakes committed by Hank and Elaine, but there are many ways to foul up a marriage besides "committing adultery" with a softball diamond. Just how does a couple build a marriage that is safe from the many subtle dangers that are part of living in a secular, sex-soaked society? How do two people learn to be "happy though married," and avoid divorce?

The best way to prevent divorce is to prepare for marriage. Too simple an answer? Maybe, but one of the big problems with marriages today, one of the reasons why over one million men and women went into the divorce courts in 1967, is that too many of them married without having any real clue about what they were doing or how to go about it.

Not that people don't know about the birds and the bees. The trouble is, too many couples know so little about much else. They lack a healthy and balanced view of sex and sexuality. To use marriage only as a legal excuse to hop in bed is to profane a holy gift of God.

Today, many young couples are marching to the

GENERATIONS WHO HAVE GROWN UP ON TV HAVE BEEN "PROGRAMMED" TO ASSOCIATE LOVE WITH PHYSICAL ATTRACTION.

altar with a concept of love and marriage that has been molded by watching thousands of hours of television programs and commercials. Unconsciously, they associate love with physical attraction, that "certain something" that draws a man and a woman together. But what is drawn together by physical attraction can easily come apart, unless there is the cement of real love, the cement of unselfishly caring about each other.

All right then, what is this "real love"? How do you find it? How do you keep it? Most important, how do you prepare for a marriage that has "real love"?

You can start preparing for marriage by seeking to become the most mature person you possibly can be. You become mature by realizing that while there is a physical side to marriage and being "turned on" biologically, there are also the spiritual and psychological sides of married life. God made human beings this way and ironically enough, if a couple doesn't have spiritual and psychological compatibility, the physical side of marriage is often a lot less than it is advertised to be.

In marriage, two people become "one" in every sense of the word. That is why Gen. 2:24 uses the term "one flesh." By "one flesh" the Bible not only means becoming one physically in the act of sexual intercourse. "One flesh" also means becoming one in mind and spirit. In the Hebrew language of the Old Testament, "flesh" stands for the whole of a person's life, including feelings, aspirations, strengths and weaknesses.*

"Making up in bed" doesn't always work

A lot of couples scrap and fight and then hope that they can "make up in bed." But sex is no "magic band aid" that you can apply to the psychological cuts and bruises that are bound to occur in any marriage. On the contrary, those psychological cuts and bruises are exactly what prevent a lot of husbands and wives from knowing the true joy of giving themselves completely to each other in sex. And so, the vicious circle gets more vicious. Because they aren't getting along at the dinner table or in the car or over the phone, they don't get along in bed and thus the rift widens further and further.

What is the big secret to this business of "getting along" and enjoying "real love"?

It might help to see the marriage bond as a rope (no, not something to use to go hang yourself, but something to bind you to your partner). This rope has at least five main strands: being able to communicate with one another; appreciating each other;

*"Sex in a Theological Perspective," Donald Bastian, *Christianity Today,* July 18, 1968, p. 8.

THE MARRIAGE BOND HAS FIVE STRANDS

having consideration for one another; participating in life together; loving and serving God together.

If you apply these five strands of the marriage bond to Hank and Elaine, it is not too hard to see what went wrong with their marriage.

First, there is this matter of learning to communicate with one another. There is a lot of talk about communication today. That's the problem. There is more talk than communicating. A basic cause of marital troubles today is lack of communication. One partner wants to share an important idea, but the other is "too busy to listen."

Learning to communicate is not easy. One misconception is that you have to be a "good talker" in order to communicate. Actually, it is of much more value to be a good listener. Really try to hear what the other person is trying to say. Let him or her know that you believe you understand what he is trying to say and that you respect and accept his views and ideas.

Communication obviously broke down between

Elaine and Hank because there was no sharing. Hank was "too busy" to really concern himself about how his wife really felt or what she really wanted. Hank was interested in what Hank wanted. It is easy to see that Elaine soon felt that she was not being appreciated

A basic pitfall in marriage is that wives don't feel appreciated by their husbands and vice versa.

"He never appreciates all the cooking and house cleaning I do."

"She never appeciates how hard I have to work to pay the bills."

Taking your mate for granted is selfish

And so it goes. The opposite of appreciating one another is "taking each other for granted." Taking someone for granted is a selfish act. It means that you prefer to use the other person as a "thing" that was designed for your convenience rather than seeing that person as someone to be loved.

It didn't take Elaine long to feel that she was completely unappreciated. Hank probably did appreciate the fact that she went to work to get him through school and that she was a good cook and housekeeper. But he was so wrapped up in his own little world of activities and interests that he failed to communicate to his wife that he appreciated her.

Marriage counselors often hear: "Well, of course, she *knows* I appreciate her. She *knows* I really love her. What's the matter with her anyway?"

It's a funny thing about "real love." The Bible makes it plain that marriage is a "one shot deal." Marriage is "for keeps." You only say your marriage

WHATEVER HAPPENED TO SIR GALAHAD?

vows once, but it does not follow that you tell your spouse, "I love you, honey" on your wedding day and then go through life uttering nothing more affectionate than an occasional grunt. Marriage partners need to be told and told often that they are loved. It's the considerate thing to do.

A marriage that includes loving, thoughtful consideration sees each partner patiently and courteously putting the other one first. During dating days, the fellow opens the door for the girl, helps her on with her coat, etc. But after a few months of marriage (a few weeks?) the "Sir Galahad" who would have gladly sprawled in the mud puddle and let his love walk to dry ground now lets her wade through on her own and wonders why she can't be "quick about it."

For some reason, many a husband decides that the courtesies that he showed during courtship are passé and even "corny." But real love isn't "corny" and it isn't discourteous. Real love is a tender plant that needs to be cultivated, and one of the best ways to cultivate real love is with consideration—caring about the other person's needs. In marriage, real love means putting your partner first.

In the case of Elaine and Hank it's obvious who Hank was putting first. Hank continually comes off as the "villain" in this unmellow marital drama. Keep in mind, however, that while Hank was certainly at fault, Elaine's reaction, which finally resulted in her leaving him for a short time, was hardly an example of how to be considerate, appreciative or communicative.

You may feel that Elaine was "justified" and that Hank got what "he deserved." The trouble with Elaine's response, however, was that she didn't love Hank "in spite of his faults" but she simply struck back at him out of self-pity and utter frustration.

"Putting each other first" takes practice

The reason a lot of marriage partners don't seem to be able to put each other first is that they get so little practice. They fail to really participate together in much of anything except arguing. The Bible's arithmetic says that one plus one equals one —one flesh. But too many marriages are marred by a routine that takes one partner in one direction and the other partner in the other. Many couples realize that he has his interests and she has hers, but they should also realize that love flourishes best when marriage partners share common interests.

The tragedy of having nothing more in common than talking about banalities like "how many miles do we get on the Volkswagen," is all too real in many marriages. It was all too real for Hank and Elaine. Elaine wanted to do things with Hank, but Hank was too busy worrying about his batting average. All the while, he was striking out at home.

Christian couples have power if . . .

Ironically enough, Hank and Elaine apparently had a "Christian marriage." At least they both were church members and Hank was a stalwart on the Sunday school teaching staff. Because they were believers in Christ, Hank and Elaine had tremendous power available to them to help build real love into their marriage. The question is, *did they use that power?*

As is the case with many a Christian couple, Hank and Elaine "missed the spiritual boat completely." They had God's directions for marriage—in the Scriptures—but they didn't use them.* They depended, rather haphazardly, on their own mental, physical and psychological abilities to make their marriage work, and they forgot that in Christ they had unlimited resources for guidance and wisdom.

When two Christians enter into marriage as God planned it, they have a life-time of opportunities to help each other grow spiritually. When they are truly "one in Christ," they open their lives to Him and together they become aware of their spiritual needs and the responsibilities in their home.

Actually, being dedicated to Christ is the central strand in the bond of marriage. If a couple will start with this, if each partner will confess his petty,

*See, for example, the "Take Time . . ." study on Ephesians 5, p. 191.

childish and immature habits and faults before God and before his spouse, then the rest of the strands of the marriage bond twist firmly into place. That couple will communicate. They will appreciate each other and be considerate of each other, and it goes without saying that they will be participating together in the ebb and flow of real life.

It would be interesting to see what a change could be wrought in the Christian families and churches across America if young couples would at least put these five strands—communication, appreciation, consideration, participation, and above all, dedication to Christ—*at least on an equal* basis with physical attraction in order to decide "Are we really in love?"

Marriage is "for adults only"

Everyone recalls those famous words intoned solemnly by the minister: ". . . to have and to hold from this day forward, for better or for worse, for richer or for poorer, in sickness and in health, to love and to cherish, until death do us part."

The challenge in these familiar lines is definitely not for children. Childhood is a time for irresponsibility. Growing up means becoming able to take on responsibility, and marriage means responsibility, not the legalization of "recreational sex."

There are too many "little boys and little girls" who are marching to the altar, only to find that six months or possibly six years later they "don't want to play this game anymore." And so, they do what children usually do: they "gather their toys and go home"—they get a divorce.

Playboys make good marriage partners (?)

Playboy likes to claim that if a man will live like a playboy in his teens and 20's, he will make an excellent marriage partner in his 30's and 40's. *Playboy's* argument runs something like this: "Why should people be forced into marriages when they're too young, have too little money, or when they aren't ready to really settle down? If people will live as we suggest, they can have their pleasures while they're young and save marriage for when they are older, more mature, and ready to take on responsibility."

This argument sounds appealing—until you start to analyze it. By what twist of logic can it be determined that living a life dedicated to "I'll take if you'll give" makes a person into the mature individual he needs to be in order to cope with the responsibilities of marriage? By what strange twist of logic can *Playboy's* policy of "dog eat dog with hearts and flowers" develop people with the character and the commitment needed to make marriage work?

It is ironic that *Playboy's* answer to the mistakes and sin that have ruined many a marriage is a way of life filled with even more mistakes and sin. The things that really bug people ... the things that destroy marriages ... are the things that have always ruined human relationships ever since Cain clobbered Abel: dishonesty, jealousy, cheating, selfishness, greed, lust, self-centeredness. *Playboy's* answer to the problems that destroy many a marriage is to engage in a pursuit of pleasure that has premarital sex as first priority. The inevitable result

is the rationalization and justification of cheating, dishonesty, lust, greed and self-centeredness.

There is an old saying that might be worth pondering to those who are sincere about preparing for marriage: "Until you stop banging on your high chair, don't risk becoming a daddy."

TAKE TIME...

Use the following ideas to take time to apply the Bible to your life and any situations you face.

Blueprint for a successful marriage

Although divorce rates are soaring, many people do make a success out of marriage and live happy, fulfilled lives. Among those who are the happiest are couples who experience the truth of Eph. 5:21-33, which not only speaks of the wonderful mysteries of Christ's love for His church, but which also gives a practical outline of how two people can find ultimate joy in a marriage relationship.

²¹"Honor Christ by submitting to each other. ²²You wives must submit to your husband's leadership in the same way you submit to the Lord. ²³For a husband is in charge of his wife in the same way Christ is in charge of His body the church. (He gave His very life to take care of it and be its Savior!) ²⁴So you wives must willingly obey your husbands in everything, just as the church obeys Christ. ²⁵And you husbands, show the same kind of love to your wives as Christ showed to the church when He died for her, ²⁶To make her holy and clean, washed by baptism and God's Word; ²⁷So that He could give her to Himself as a glorious church without a single spot or wrinkle or any other blemish, being holy and without a single fault. ²⁸That is how husbands should treat their wives, loving them as parts of themselves. For since a man and his wife are now one, a man is really doing himself a favor and loving himself when he loves his wife! ²⁹,³⁰No one hates his own body but lovingly cares for it, just as Christ cares for His body the church, of which we are parts. ³¹(That the husband and wife are one body is proved by the Scripture which says, 'A man must leave his father and mother when he marries, so that he can be perfectly joined to his wife, and the two shall be one.') ³²I know this is hard to understand, but it is an illustration of the way we are part of the body of Christ. ³³So again I say, a man must love his wife as a part of himself; and the wife must see to it that she deeply respects her husband—obeying, praising and honoring him" (Eph. 5:21-33, *Living New Testament*).

Why is "submitting to each other" so important in marriage?

Why does a man really do himself a favor when he loves his wife as he loves himself?

In what way would you say that marriage is an illustration of the way Christians are "part of the body of Christ?"

Do you think that reading this passage together regularly would help a Christian couple have a better marriage? Why?

TAKE INVENTORY . . .

The last two chapters have talked a lot about marriage, but marriage is not necessarily for everyone. Are you willing to settle for the single life, if that seems to be what God wants for you? Think carefully before you answer.

Some of the wisest words on "real love" ever written came from the pen of C. S. Lewis who said:

" . . . love is not merely a feeling. It is a deep unity, maintained by the will and deliberately strengthened by habit: reinforced by (in Christian marriages) the grace which both partners ask, and receive, from God. They can have this love for each other even at those moments when they do not like each other; as you love yourself even when you do not like yourself. They can retain this love even when each would easily, if they allowed themselves, be "in love" with someone else. "Being in love" first moved them to promise fidelity: this quieter love then enables them to keep the promise. It is on this love that the engine of marriage is run: being in love was the explosion that started it."*

Analyze what Lewis has written. Do you believe that you could have love for someone even at those moments when you would not like him (or her)? Do you think this kind of love is absolutely necessary in the marriage relationship? Why?

TAKE ACTION . . .

If you want to know more about developing "real love" in a marriage relationship, the following two books offer practical advice:

Letters to Karen, Charlie W. Shedd. Copyright 1965, Abingdon Press. Dr. Shedd has been a Presbyterian minister for over 25 years and has counseled thousands of couples before and after marriage. He wrote this

Mere Christianity, C. S. Lewis, The Macmillan Co., Paperback edition, 1960, p. 99.

book for his daughter who had asked him to tell her how she could keep her husband loving her forever.

Letters to Phillip (On how to treat a woman), Charlie W. Shedd. Copyright 1968, Doubleday and Company. Dr. Shedd wrote this sequel to *Letters to Karen* when one of his four sons came to him a few weeks before his marriage and asked him for some ideas on how to be a good husband. Easy reading—and excellent.

There are two short sentences that could do a lot to improve the atmosphere in many marriages. These sentences are: "I was wrong" and "I am sorry." If you happen to be married, try using them more often (along with another sure-fire standby, "I sure do love you").

If you're not married, you don't have to wait until you find a husband or wife to practice things like: "I was wrong" and "I'm sorry." Chances are you could put these two little phrases to work right now at home, at school, at work, etc. Try it and see what happens. If you are going quite steadily with someone or if engaged, get together with that person and discuss Eph. 5:21-33. Also discuss the key elements for putting real love into marriage that this chapter deals with: communication, appreciation, consideration, participation and dedication to Christ.

CHAPTER 11

What the world needs now is...

What does the world *really* need?

The popular song writer of the middle 1960's was never so right: this battered, embattled world . . . this planet that faces annihilation through a nuclear holocaust or overpopulation starvation . . . needs "love, sweet love."

People talk a lot about love. They talk about loving one another and loving their enemies. They talk about loving God and loving their neighbor. They talk about love for mankind.

What does the Bible say about love? Christians do a lot of talking about love. What do they mean? For one thing, the Bible describes love as a "more excellent way" to do things than people normally follow. The "normal and natural" approach to life is selfishness and self-centeredness—the law of self-preservation.

It is perfectly natural to think of yourself first, but a world full of people thinking of themselves first is exactly why the world faces the problems it faces today.

In I Cor. 13:1-3 Paul makes it clear what love is not:

[1]"If I had the gift of being able to speak in other languages without learning them, and could speak in every language there is in all of heaven and earth, but didn't love others, I would only be making noise. [2]If I had the gift of prophecy and knew all about what is going to happen in the future, knew everything about *everything*, but didn't love others, what good would it do? Even if I had the gift of faith so that I could speak to a mountain and make it move, I would still be worth nothing at all without love. [3]If I gave everything I have to poor people, and if I were burned alive for preaching the Gospel but didn't love others, it would be of no value whatever" (I Cor. 13:1-3, *Living New Testament*).

One way to sum up these verses is to say that love is not "being a phony."

No matter what your relationship might be with another person, without love, sweet talk, brilliant oratory, "great faith," and even "generous giving" are of little use or value. A relationship without love is like running a high powered racing engine without oil. You might have the best engineered racing motor in the world. You might have the best parts, the best materials, the best workmanship, but without oil, friction will soon cause that motor to burn up and fly to pieces.

The same is true with people. Without love to oil the inevitable friction in a human relationship, you're asking for disaster. Divorce cases are casualties caused by lack of the "oil of love."

Since Paul tells us what love *is* not, he is obligated to tell us what he thinks love really *is*, and he does so:

"'Love is very patient and kind, never jealous or envious, never boastful or proud, 'Never haughty or selfish or rude. Love does not demand its own way. It is not irritable or touchy. It does not hold grudges and will hardly even notice when others do it wrong" (I Cor. 13:4,5, *Living New Testament*).

This brief series of staccato-like phrases adds up to one basic idea: "Love is being able to take it" (and that doesn't mean the kind of "taking" the new morality promotes).

Go back and look at v. 5 again and consider all of the ideas that are there. Are these ideas compatible with the "free fornication" urged by *Playboy*? Are they compatible with Joseph Fletcher's situation ethics, which would see fit to excuse fornication, adultery and even murder as long as you can say sincerely that you "did it in love"?

Behind every act of fornication and adultery is the basic attitude "I want, I need, I deserve it, I can't live without it, I'll take it!" If anybody is "demanding his own way" it is the fornicator or the adulterer. Joseph Fletcher would have you believe that a husband can express "*agape* love" by being unfaithful to his wife. If this is *agape*, it's rather *sloppy*. As William Banowsky aptly points out, there are some acts that are so inconsistent with *agape* love that they must always be branded wrong and never right.*

If love means anything, it means being able to take it, and being able to take it means being able to put up with something that is a little less than you would like to have. It means denying yourself; yes, it means suffering.

Playboy magazine makes the asinine charge that anyone who puts self-denial ahead of self-gratifica-

*The New Morality: A Christian Solution, William Banowsky. Copyright 1968, Campus Evangelism, published by R. B. Sweet Co., Inc., p. 15.

LOVE IS "HANGING IN THERE"

tion is a masochist*—someone who enjoys being kicked around. But the real point about suffering as far as the Christian is concerned is that he doesn't necessarily enjoy it, but he endures it for a higher cause and a deeper purpose.

The person who wants to "love," says Paul, is not only able to "take it." He is also able to "hang in there":

"It is never glad about injustice, but rejoices whenever truth wins out. 'If you love someone you will be loyal to him no matter what the cost. You will always . . . stand your ground in defending him" (I Cor. 13:6,7, *Living New Testament*).

Purveyors of various brands of the new morality—Hugh Hefner's or Joseph Fletcher's—speak much about being against injustice. Yet, Hefner's "no deposit, no return" philosophy of cohabitation speaks for itself. Glorifying fornication and winking

---

*Perhaps you have heard the joke: "Hurt me, hurt me," cried the masochist. "No, no," said the sadist.

at adultery will never help the world discover what it means to love, to have mercy, to seek justice. Fornication and adultery are acts based upon selfishness, and selfishness is the corrosive acid that eats at the vitals of human relationships.

Nor does the situation ethics brand of the new morality do any better. It is all well and good to talk about love being your "only real motive," but the new moralists make sure that they retain the authority and the right to decide just what is a "loving act."

In effect, they play judge and jury and disperse justice as they see fit. They practice a brand of ethics that makes it easy to confuse "justice" with personal convenience, or the "practical way out."

The cross was not a convenient "way out" . . .

But for the committed Christian, the Bible makes one thing very clear: love is something that involves a lot more than "personal convenience" or a "practical solution to a sticky problem." Dying on the cross wasn't exactly the most "convenient" way out of Jesus' disagreement with the religious establishment.

God's love is needed today in Christian families as well as non-Christian. God's love is needed today between the generations, where a communication gap seems to grow wider by the minute. God's love is needed between groups, organizations, nations and races.

The "real love" of I Corinthians is certainly needed by husbands and wives. How many divorces could be avoided if couples married realizing that real love is *giving to* one another instead of *getting from* one another?

"Real love" in marriage includes two vital elements: unconditional acceptance of the other person, plus a creative quality in the relationship.

Many people marry someone and try to assure themselves that they accept them the way that they are, but they have a hidden agenda. Many people have the idea that they are going to run a rehabilitation center with a clientele of one—their husband (or wife). This just doesn't work. The basic desire to change someone (meaning trying to get someone to act in a way that is more agreeable to you) is a hostile desire. You can cover up this hostility by saying that you are doing it for his or her own good, but you are actually doing it for your own good and your own convenience.

But if you really accept someone, there will be a creativity in your relationship. You will accept them unconditionally and leave yourself with a much better chance of really being patient, really being kind, truly lacking jealousy and pride. You will have a much better possibility of not being proud, haughty, rude, touchy, irritable or holding grudges (remembering those times when your lover "did you dirt").

How do you achieve this magnificent condition known as "unconditionally accepting the other person?" You get it from the One who unconditionally accepts all mankind. You learn how to love from God, and as you learn how to love from God you learn how to love your husband or wife. You seek to make your relationship creative, not destructive.

When you love "destructively," you want to change your mate to suit your preferences and your tastes. When you love your mate "creatively," you are able to take it when things do not go perfectly. You are able to "hang-in-there" when you face disappointments and frustrations. God doesn't give us creative love for one another overnight, but He is working in us to will and do of His good pleasure (Phil. 2:13) and to make us into all that we can possibly be (Rom. 5:2, *Living New Testament*).

Can love span the generation gap?

The "real love" of I Corinthians 13 is certainly needed between the generations today. The "communication gap" is well-known—in families, on high school and college campuses, in companies, organizations and institutions of all kinds. Readers of this book are either under or over the much maligned age of 30. The cry of the "now" generation is, "you can't trust anyone over 30." Whom do *you* trust? Whom do *you* fear? Where will it all end? Will teen-agers take over and ship all adults to LSD farms as they did in *Wild in the Streets?*

How long will the "under 30" generation hide behind the hypocritical excuse that the "establishment is phony" and that only youth is looking for honesty and reality? How long will the "over 30" generation hide its own hypocrisy behind the cry of, "You must show respect for law and order"? (The young person's sense of ethics and attitude toward law and order is bred into him from the cradle. If his home has real respect for law and order, he usually will too.)

IS EITHER SIDE LISTENING?

One key source of trouble between the generations is that *neither side is really trying to listen to the other.* Instead of exchanging views, they exchange insults. Instead of talking and thinking together, the older and younger generations stay in their respective camps and do a lot of imagining about what each is saying about the other. Both sides refuse to admit that their generations need each other. They refuse to see that to go on with bickering, misunderstanding and even hatred is a cancerous condition that can only lead to destruction.*

*This is not to say that a great deal of the rioting and student take-overs on the campuses in recent years was not the work of professional agitators. There is also little doubt that many of these agitators owe their allegiance to Communism. But blaming all the riots and demonstrations on Communists is too simple. The generation gap usually goes right back into the home. How many student demonstrators could have said that they were "getting along splendidly" with their parents? The generation gap in the home sowed the discord and the college campus reaped the strife.

Shall love overcome?

The real love of I Corinthians 13 is certainly needed between the races—particularly the black and the white. Too many white middle class Christians are very much like the only swimmer in a crowd watching the struggles of a drowning man. They won't dive in because he might pull them under too. Or they are like a doctor during an epidemic who won't give the necessary medicine for fear of catching a disease.

White Christians have the reconciliation serum, but it's no good if they don't deliver it personally in Jesus' name. A Black Power conference held in Newark, New Jersey in 1967 placed Christianity (as the Black Power advocates saw it) at the head of the list of enemies of the black man.*

What's the answer? To paraphrase Ken Taylor's paraphrase of I John 3:18, "It's time for the white Christian to stop saying he 'loves the black man just as much as anybody else' and instead start to show it by his actions." And the same can be said for the black believer, who may feel that he's all out of cheeks to turn. Tremendous strides in healing the horrible rift in race relations could be taken if black and white Christians would make a real attempt to get to know one another.**

The percentage of Negroes who subscribe to the ideas of Black Power has been small, but it can

---

*"Apart Hate," John Goodwin, *Eternity*, August, 1968. pp. 10, 11. The entire issue is excellent for its practical suggestions on building understanding between blacks and whites.

**For practical ideas on how to go about this, see "Take Action..." p. 206.

grow. And it will grow unless white Christians take a step toward and over the wall that separates them from the black race, and from any race for that matter. Prejudice and racism is not limited to black and white; there are lots of other colors in the scene as well.

No matter where you look—what the world needs now is love, God's love. Paul said it all long ago: "There are three things that remain—faith, hope and love—and the greatest of these is love" (I Cor. 13:13, *Living New Testament*).

TAKE TIME . . .

Read I Cor. 13:1-7,13 and use the following ideas to take time to apply the Bible to your life and any situations you face.

Love is a very specific thing

¹"If I had the gift of being able to speak in other languages without learning them, and could speak in every language there is in all of heaven and earth, but didn't love others, I would only be making noise. ²If I had the gift of prophecy and knew all about what is going to happen in the future, knew everything about *everything*, but didn't love others, what good would it do? Even if I had the gift of faith so that I could speak to a mountain and make it move, I would still be worth nothing at all without love. ³If I gave everything I have to poor people, and if I were burned alive for preaching the Gospel but didn't love others, it would be of no value whatever. ⁴Love is very patient and kind, never jealous or envious, never boastful or proud, ⁵Never haughty or selfish or rude. Love does not demand its own way. It is not irritable or touchy. It does not hold grudges and will hardly even notice when others do it

wrong. ⁶It is never glad about injustice, but rejoices whenever truth wins out. ⁷If you love someone you will be loyal to him no matter what the cost. You will always believe in him, always expect the best of him, and always stand your ground in defending him . . . ¹³There are three things that remain—faith, hope, and love—and the greatest of these is love" (I Cor. 13:1-7, 13, *Living New Testament*).

Write out your own check list of the specific qualities of love that Paul lists. Compare this check list with your own feelings toward your family or friends, people you know, organizations, other races, etc.

Compare I Cor. 13:1-7 with I John 3:18. Is love merely a feeling, or is it deeds and actions? Is it both? Why?

Compare I Cor. 13:1-7 with I John 4:7-20, Eph. 3:17-20. How does a Christian become a loving person? List six specific things you can do to show people close to you that you love them.

TAKE INVENTORY . . .

Jesus had one "no" in His Gospel—the "no" you must say to yourself. The paradox of Christianity is that if you say "no" to yourself and "yes" to others, you receive far more than you ever give.

Do you find this Christian paradox to be true in your life? Do you get more out of giving than receiving? Perhaps you aren't receiving much because you aren't giving much. Remember the hedonistic paradox: if you live to seek pleasure it will elude you in the long-run . . . pleasure sought is pleasure lost.

TAKE ACTION . . .

What the world needs now is love—God's love lived out in the lives of Christians who are committed to

Christ. Choose from the following projects and put God's love into action—now.

Help build a bridge of understanding across the "generation gap" by making a point of letting someone in the "other generation" (older or younger depending on who you are) know that you are interested in understanding his or her point of view.

Love and understanding between the races has become a major problem within the last several years. Here are some specific suggestions that apply to fostering better understanding between Negro and white, but they can just as easily be adapted to other race problems as well.

Read. Books by Negro evangelicals include *Shall We Overcome* by Howard Jones, *Inasmuch* by David Moberg, and *Black and Free* by Tom Skinner. Good secular books are *Crisis in Black and White, The Desegregated Heart, Black Like Me, The Other America* and *Dark Ghetto.* Also read *Ebony* or the *Negro Digest* or a Negro newspaper in your area.

Visit. Work through your pastor or youth director and see if you can arrange to visit a Negro church in your area.

Talk. If you have no friends of another race (for example, if you are a white who knows few if any Negroes), see what you can do to build some relationships. Work through churches, youth centers, YMCA's and schools in your area and make an attempt to know someone from another race. Hear them out on what they believe and what they think. Some people are bitter, but a lot more are seeking to understand, to live in peace and harmony and to carry out the Bible's clear teaching to love one another. Find at least a few of these people and start building the bridge of understanding now. Time may be running out.

CHAPTER 12

Hail to the new morality!

Yes, that's right—hail to *Playboy*, Hugh Hefner, Helen Gurley Brown, Ralph Ginzburg and other outspoken sexual revolutionaries. A toast to situation ethics—Joseph Fletcher, Bishop Robinson, Bishop Pike, Canon Rhymes, et al. All these champions of the new morality have done more for the cause of Christ than perhaps all the atheists in history.

How's that again? How can atheists do anything for Christ? How can the immoral doctrines of the new morality be of any help?

Atheists are often a help to Christianity because they are so obvious and crude. After all, Scripture says, "The fool hath said in his heart, there is no God" (Ps. 14:1). The atheist's open denial of God and Christ usually serves to strengthen the Christian's convictions (and, unfortunately, his complacency).

With the new morality, of course, the attack is

206

much different. Indeed, much of it comes from inside the church. While some of the sexual revolutionists are quite possibly atheistic or at least agnostic, many of the peddlers of the new morality are "men of the cloth." They are theologians, preachers, Bible scholars. They write and speak from a vantage point that includes long years of study. They have thought through many of the questions and have decided to come up with "new answers." They have pinpointed one of the great pitfalls in the Christian walk—becoming legalistic and hypocritical.

The Christian may not agree with the subjective subtleties of Joseph Fletcher's situation ethics or with the huffing and puffing of Hugh Hefner against the puritanical establishment, but each of these men in his own particular way and style brings the real issues out in the open for the Christian who is concerned about right and wrong.

What *do* you do with Fletcher's "sticky cases"? What do you do when you are forced into a corner where it seems that you're wrong if you do and you're wrong if you don't? Who *does* get the blood plasma—the drunken bum or the mother of three?

And what *do* you do with *Playboy's* slick, sophisticated attack on Biblical morality? What do you do with *Playboy's* indictment that labels Christianity puritanical and Victorian?

The new morality does Christians a favor

Here is the reason why the new morality has actually done Christians a favor. The new morality makes the Christian face up to legalism and hypoc-

**BEFORE CASTING THE FIRST STONE,
AT THE NEW MORALITY, THE CHRISTIAN
NEEDS TO LOOK INSIDE HIMSELF**

risy, two of the most insidious and subtle dangers to his spiritual life.

Before the Christian can first cast stones at the sexual revolutionists and the peddlers of the new morality, he needs to examine *himself*. What is his own score in the morals ball game? What about sex? What about honesty? What about truthfulness? What about loyalty? What about treating others as you would want them to treat you? What about materialism? What is really important—your own personal pleasure or that sticky item the Bible calls "discipleship"?

Make no mistake about it. The current moral crisis and sexual revolution has to separate the turncoats from those who have truly turned to Christ. A lot of people do a lot of worrying about just how "saved" they really are. They wonder if their religion really "means anything." One very real test is to start comparing your personal moral values to the clear teachings of Scripture—especially the teachings of the one whom you call your Saviour and your Lord.

What about this battle-cry of the sexual revolution: "Everybody's doing it"? Suppose Kinsey was right (it's doubtful, but possible.) Suppose *Playboy* is right and there are far more people interested in *Playboy's* point of view on sex and other pleasures than there are those who believe in chastity and Biblical morality.

So what? Is it really so surprising that the masses go for something besides what the Bible teaches? This has been the whole story of man from start to present. Man doesn't want to listen to what the Bible says. Man wants to go his own way and "do his own thing." Listening to and obeying God cramps his style.

Christ's love doesn't wink at mistakes

Christ never worried about cramping anyone's style—particularly the playboy's. He didn't try for every vote he could find. He made no deals, He made no concessions. He made no compromises. He brought love to the world, but it was real love—not the phony kind that is willing to "wink at your mistakes." And Christ's love is certainly not the artificial brand that looks down a long, blue nose, trying to find every imperfection and infraction of the rules that it can.

In many ways, the Gospel preached by Jesus Christ was the kind that won Him few friends in "the establishment," and which looked far too difficult for the masses with nothing on their minds but pleasure. Christ turned the typical concept of love

SELF LOVE IS
PERFECTLY NATURAL

"inside out." It's natural to think of loving yourself, but Jesus said to love others first. It's natural to think of what we will eat, what we will wear, where we will live, how much we will make, etc., etc., but Jesus said, "Seek ... first the kingdom of God, and his righteousness; and all these things shall be added unto you" (Matt. 6:33).

It's natural to "stand up for your rights" but Jesus taught His disciples to turn the other cheek (Matt. 5:39) and to "treat others as you want them to treat you" (Luke 6:31, *Living New Testament*).

People have a strange way of equating their morals with specific acts. Because they don't go around hitting people over the head or robbing banks or breaking windows or setting fire to ghettos, they consider themselves "quite moral." Christ saw this to be precisely the problem of His day, and that is why He went to the trouble to spell out the heart of real morality in the Sermon on the Mount.

The question is not, "Have you murdered anyone?" The question is, rather, "Have you ever been violently angry? Have you ever called someone a fool or an idiot? Have you ever cursed anyone?" (See Matt. 5:21,22, *Living New Testament.*)

The question is not "Have you committed adultery by going to bed with someone?" The question is, rather, "Have you lusted in your heart?" (See Matt. 5:27-30, *Living New Testament.*)

What Jesus did was to tell us that morality is not a list of do's and don'ts. Morality is not a code as much as it is a condition. The attitude of love for others.

So what is a Christian to do—toss out all codes and hope for the best? That would be no real answer, and furthermore it is impossible. All of us live according to some kind of code. For all of his condemning of code ethics and legalism, even Joseph Fletcher has a personal moral code which he calls "the law of love." And even Hugh Hefner has a moral code of sorts: Do unto others before they do unto you—just be sure that it's legal, that they are agreeable, and "nobody gets hurt."

And, a Christian must also develop his own moral code. Every Christian, in fact, is developing his or her own code, and has been ever since the cradle. But in these days of the new morality and the sexual revolution, the Christian has a unique opportunity to develop a *creative moral code based on that little item that the world has so little of: love.*

How do you develop a "creative Christian moral code?" Some ideas are in the Conclusion of this book (p. 215), but the basic foundation is in the "Take Time . . ." section of this chapter. Be sure to "take time" to think about just what it means to be a Christian. To paraphrase the old saying: "It's not

211

that Christianity was tried and found wanting, it's that Christian morality has always looked too difficult and that is why a lot of people have failed to try Christianity."

More precisely, people have failed to really try Jesus Christ. Christianity is not "living by a rule-book." Doing the right thing is not blind, slavish obedience to the Ten Commandments. Christianity is not legalism.

Christianity is Jesus Christ. Christianity is knowing Christ as Saviour and obeying Him as Lord. That, as they say, is what it's "all about."

TAKE TIME . . .

Use the following ideas to take time to apply the Bible to your life and any situation you face.

It helps to be a Christian . . .

When it comes to practicing Christian ethics, it helps to be a Christian. That sounds a little too obvious to even mention, but keep in mind that the new morality has arisen to take the place of the "old morality" which is a form of Christian ethics that is long on legalism and short on personal knowledge of Jesus Christ. Following are some key passages from Scripture that explain just what a Christian believes and who a Christian really knows:

[21,22]"But now God has shown us a different way to heaven—not by 'being good enough' and trying to keep His laws, but by a new way (though not new, really, for the Scriptures told about it long ago). Now God says He will accept and acquit us—declare us 'Not guilty'—if we trust Jesus Christ to take away our sins. And we all can be saved in this same way, by coming to Christ, no matter who we are or what we have been like.

²³"Yes, all have sinned; all fall short of God's glorious ideal; ²⁴Yet now God declares us 'not guilty' of offending Him if we trust in Jesus Christ, who in His kindness freely takes away our sins" (Rom. 3:21-24, *Living New Testament*).

"When someone becomes a Christian he becomes a brand new person inside. He is not the same any more. A new life has begun!" (II Cor. 5:17, *Living New Testament*).

⁹"For if you tell others with your own mouth that Jesus Christ is your Lord, and believe in your own heart that God has raised Him from the dead, you will be saved. ¹⁰For it is by believing in his heart that a man becomes right with God; and with his mouth he tells others of his faith, confirming his salvation" (Rom. 10:9,10, *Living New Testament.*)

⁸"Because of His kindness you have been saved through trusting Christ. And even trusting is not of yourselves; it too is a gift from God. ⁹Salvation is not a reward for the good we have done, so none of us can take any credit for it. ¹⁰It is God Himself who has made us what we are and given us new lives from Christ Jesus; and long ages ago He planned that we should spend these lives in helping others" (Eph. 2:8-10, *Living New Testament*).

From what you read in these verses, what would you say is really involved in being a Christian? Have you taken these steps?

TAKE INVENTORY . . .

The creative Christian moral code outlined in the conclusion to *It All Depends* includes four points:
1. Treat people as persons, not things.
2. Serve God, not yourself.
3. Seek God's will, not "What is best for me?"
4. Balance love against law. (pp. 215-226)

After reading the Conclusion carefully, evaluate how you have been living in the last few weeks and months. Would you say that you have been practicing a creative Christian moral code? How does your life measure up to these four points?

TAKE ACTION ...

Read the Conclusion to this book—"Is It Worth The Risk"—especially the closing paragraphs that talk about being a "gambler for God." The Greek word is *parabolani*. Among the early Christians, the *parabolani* were those who would take any kind of personal risk to bring God's love where it was needed most.

Being against the new morality or refusing to join the sexual revolution might be good, but it won't be enough. We are too far down the toboggan chute. We need some *parabolani*. Are you willing to take the risk?

Is it worth the risk?

Let us face it. Being moral in a day when immorality is in style is risky business. You can lose everything from a girl friend or a fiancé to membership in the in-group; from a much needed raise to a desperately needed profit to keep a small business going.

The question is: "Are the losses that you might risk worth the gain that you will receive?" Following are four key thoughts to help you develop a creative Christian moral code. They are nothing new, really, but neither is the new morality. If you put these four ideas together with a genuine relationship to Jesus Christ, it just might be that you will come up with something that not only helps you know the difference between right and wrong, but something that gives you the intestinal fortitude to do something about it. First . . .

Treat people as persons, not things. Life is a

series of situations in which you have the opportunity to choose between loving people and using things or loving things and using people. For all of us the choice between right and wrong often lies in our choice of just what is more important to us— people or our own pleasures. You can lie, cheat, steal, fornicate, commit adultery, even kill, because you love some *thing* more than some *one*. The best way to avoid becoming a "people user" is to decide to . . .

Serve God, not yourself. This was precisely the choice that Jesus was offering His disciples when He included the following statement in His Sermon on the Mount: "You cannot serve two masters: God and money. For you will hate one and love the other, or else the other way around" (Matt. 6:24, *Living New Testament*).

The word used for money in the authorized version is "mammon." Actually, mammon means material things, possessions, worldly and secular values. You serve "mammon" when you are interested in satisfying only yourself. The legalist really doesn't

POINT 1—DON'T BE A PEOPLE-USER

YOU CAN'T SERVE GOD AND "MAMMON"

serve God. He serves his own particular kind of mammon—his worship of the letter of the law. As Christ told the Pharisees, they outwardly appeared righteous to men, but within they were full of hypocrisy and iniquity (Matt. 23:28).

A truly creative Christian moral code must include the responsibility to serve God.

Serving God is not a case of working your way to heaven or earning enough "brownie points" to stay in the "Christian Club." Believing in Christ means becoming part of the family of God, being "born again" through the Holy Spirit (John 3:1-8). You do not become a Christian in the same way that you join a club or a political party. To be a Christian is to follow a completely new way of life, and that brings up point three in your creative code:

You seek God's will, not "what is best for me." Advocates of the new morality say that today people are fed up with traditional codes and sets of rules. They are questioning, seeking, asking: "Is my life meaningful?"

217

The Christian has every right to question the creeds and the codes of his faith. God loves us enough to make us free persons, who can choose the way we want to go and what we want to believe. Once we have believed in Christ, there is no rule that says we can't question and evaluate the doctrines, codes and creeds of Christianity.

It is perfectly natural and perfectly in order for the Christian to ask if the Ten Commandments are valid and relevant for this day and age. But there are two basic ways to question your Christian faith: destructively or constructively. If your Christianity is little more than creeds or codes, you might decide to question it destructively. You will question it in a way that will not only breed doubt, but nourish it as well. If, however, your Christianity is based upon a personal relationship to Christ, then you can question the creeds and codes of your faith in a constructive way.

Ask not, "What is best for me?"

As he evaluates Biblical morality and the "Biblical code" the person who really knows Christ is not asking, "What is the best thing for me?" Instead he is asking, "What is God's will?"

Perhaps the question that Christians ask most often is "How can I know God's will for me?" *Wanting to do God's will* is a great part of the battle. If you want to know God's will, if you want to obey God and serve Him only, you will find guidance and answers you need for life. You will also find the key to Christian ethics and you will know

YOU DON'T GAIN SELF-CONTROL BY "THINKING GOOD THOUGHTS"

the real difference between right and wrong.*

Perhaps you have noticed in these first three points on a creative Christian moral code that the element of "self-control" is central. You need self-control to treat people as persons and not as things. You need self-control to serve God and not self. You need self-control if you are interested in seeking God's will and not just your own will.

There is a paradox here, however. The Christian does not go around saying, "I've got to control myself. I've got to think good thoughts. I've got to be Godly." Many of the religions and sects of the world are based on the idea of meditation, thinking yourself into a certain state of mind, thinking positive thoughts, etc.

But for the Christian, *self-control means to be controlled by Christ*. This mysterious element—being controlled by Christ through the power of the

*For Scriptural teachings on knowing God's will, see Ps. 48:14; 143:10; Matt. 12:50; John 7:17; Rom. 12:2; Eph. 6:6; James 4:15.

Holy Spirit—is why Christianity towers over all other faiths and all other ethical systems.* The Holy Spirit is the one who helps you . . .

Balance love against law. Remember the "archway to Christian ethics" in Chapter 5? The blocks making up the sides of the arch are the Ten Commandments, but as any builder will tell you, the "keystone"—the stone that lies directly in the center of the top of the arch—is the all-important item.

Without the keystone, the arch will collapse and crumble to the ground. In this illustration, of course, the "keystone" is the "rock of love." Without love, you are left desperately trying to "hold up the Ten Commandments all by yourself."

This happens to a lot of Christians. Along with accepting Christ, they accept the "list of do's and don'ts." Instead of concentrating on Christ, they concentrate on their list. With iron discipline and admirable resolve, they try to "hold up their end of

*Scriptural passages dealing with the power of the Holy Spirit include Rom. 8:1-11 and Gal. 5:16-25.

the deal." They try their best to "live like Christians." The result of trying to "live like a Christian" is to wind up a legalist.

The old cliché says "charity begins at home." You might rewrite that to say, "Christianity begins with Christ, not rules." A nice tidy little list of do's and don'ts will never bring your through those sticky situations in life where you have to choose between the lesser of two evils. You can face those sticky situations with Christ, or you can leave Him at home —back in the drawer with your unused Bible and your other souvenirs. If you face this sticky problem with Christ, you are not left with the choice of the believer in situation ethics who says that people no longer ask "What are the rules of my religion?" but "What is right for me?" As a Christian, you do not ask "What is right for me?" but you ask, "What does Christ want me to do?"

Sticky situations aren't quite so sticky if . . .

This isn't easy to do, but it's strange that when you do do it, the sticky situations somehow aren't quite so sticky anymore. Furthermore, if you have to choose between the "lesser of two evils" you know you have done so by trusting yourself to God's grace and mercy. You are not happy about choosing the "lesser evil" and you certainly don't try to justify it as something right and good because you have rationalized in your own mind that this was the best way to show love.

In many cases where it appears that you have to break one law to keep another, it is only another example of how God uses the law to show you that you are human, fallible and quite incapable of living a life with a perfect moral score. The Scriptures teach us that the law is our school master to bring us to Christ. Christ is the key to a creative moral code. Any other approach leads into legalism, lawlessness or the "slough of situational despond."

But "creative codes" don't decrease the risks

A "creative code" built on Christ is great to have, but you might as well face facts. Walking with Christ *is* risky. Christianity is a gamble in a way. But then, so is life.

The early Christians knew that their faith was risky. They knew that "believing in Christ" and publicly testifying of that belief was not exactly the way to "get ahead" in the pagan society in which they lived. Yet, they did it because they knew Christ was worth far more than any degree of success in a pagan secular society. They were willing to put everything on the line for Christ.

In some of the early Christian churches, there were groups that called themselves *parabolani*. This Greek word, *parabolani,* literally refers to "gambling." But the Christians who went by this name weren't running point spreads on the local chariot races, nor were they sitting up all night in games of five-card stud. Alternate meanings of *parabolani* are: "To risk, to hazard." In other words, to be a *parabolani* meant that you were willing to "take your chances for Christ."

The *parabolani* Christians would go out to the prisons and dungeons where all kinds of desperate, and even depraved and demented prisoners were kept. Without regard for personal safety, they would go in and minister to some of these criminals, some of whom were even psychopathic maniacs.

The parabolani believers also did a lot of work with those who were sick. For example, in 252 A.D., Carthage, prominent African city on the shores of the Mediterranean, was struck by a deadly plague. Dead bodies piled up in the streets, and naturally, this only helped to spread the plague more quickly. Carthage appeared doomed. Then a call came out from the Christian Bishop, Cyprian, for Christian believers to form a squad of *parabolani* who would hazard their lives in an attempt to clean up the city. The Christians responded and they came in to bury the dead bodies that were piling up in the streets. They did their best for those still sick with the plague and at the risk of their own lives they managed to save the city of Carthage from total annihilation.

"Will the real 'parabolani' please stand up?"

Perhaps the moral crisis that the churches face today is God's way of asking "the real *parabolani* to please stand up." The Christian church has an abundance of committees and enough programming to make a computer dizzy. But the church today has few *parabolani*—those willing to "play it a little bit unsafe" for Christ.

Now this might not necessarily mean dashing off to find yourself a plague where you could courageously bury the bodies of the dead and help the sick and the dying back to health. Plagues are a bit in short supply due to improved technology. But

223

there are plenty of things you can do, and the moral chaos caused by the "new morality" presents daily opportunities. Maybe it's time for more Christians to "risk" censure and disapproval by refusing to go along with the typical secular attitude that winks at rules and chuckles uproariously at double-edged jokes that are fit only for "mature audiences."

Maybe it's time for Christians to stop talking about love and start taking a few psychological risks in order to be loving. Yes, to love often means taking a risk. After all, you can get walked on, chewed out, insulted and get your feelings hurt in many ways. But isn't that what "being loving" is really all about?

"If you love only those who love you . . ."

Isn't being loving simply the task of reaching out in concern and compassion and interest to others regardless of how they will respond to you? As Christ pointed out, "If you love only those who love you, what good is that? Even scoundrels do that much" (Matt. 5:46, *Living New Testament*).

This business of "loving only those who love you back" is precisely what is behind the problems the world faces today. Christians are separated—parted by fear and hatred—because they prefer to love only "their own kind," their own color, their own social equals, their own type, their "own generation." But Christianity is an equation that has the widest possible common denominator—love.

This book opened by asking, "Is morality making its last stand?"

From the looks of things, morality is not only

making its last stand but ammunition is getting low and there is no cavalry just over the hill to ride to the rescue.

But the Christian isn't really looking for any last minute rescues or "eleventh hour reprieves." The Christian is ready to fight the battle of morality to the finish. The Christian's leader is Jesus Christ, and *Jesus Christ has never lost a moral battle.* Not that the Christian "uses Christ" as some sort of super-talisman to ward off the evil spirits and come through the war unscathed.

Christ is not your "body guard"

The Christian doesn't follow Christ for "self-protection" or for what he can get out of it. He follows Christ for what he can *put into it*—namely, himself. The answer to "being moral"—in your home, on a date, in the locker room, on the job, in class, and above all in the inner sanctum of your own soul—is found in these words:

... As an act of intelligent worship, ... give ... your bodies, as a living sacrifice, consecrated to him and acceptable by him. Don't let the world around you squeeze you into its own mold, but let God remold your minds from within, so you will learn from your own experience how His ways will really satisfy you" (Rom. 12:1,2, combination of *Phillips Translation* and *Living New Testament* paraphrases).

An act of intelligent worship ... a college girl wrote home to her father and told him about the casual approach to sex taken by many of her classmates. She was being pressured to throw away her moral standards—not only by the young men but also by the "open-minded" girls in the dorm.

225

"I haven't bought their arguments yet," she wrote, "but I must confess that there are times when I wonder what I am waiting for."

Her father wrote back and said, "I think I can tell you in six words what you are waiting for; *you are waiting to be free.* Free from the nagging voice of conscience and the grey shadow of guilt. Free to give all of yourself, not a panicky fraction. Tell your open-minded friends not to be so open-minded that their brains fall out!"

Learn from your own experience ... this is where you have to make your own private stand in the war of right and wrong. Of course, there's always the "no sweat" approach. You can be putty. You can let the world squeeze you into its own mold. It's a safe way to fly, but not very satisfying.

There is also God's way—letting him mold your mind from within, which isn't easy, and it isn't comfortable. If you stand with Christ, it's possible that you can even get hurt. After all, He did. God doesn't promise you anything—except that His ways will really satisfy you.

Is it worth the risk?

It all depends ...

Christianity and Hedonism...

A Clash of Philosophies

On October 8, 1967, William Banowsky,* who was then minister at the Broadway Church of Christ, Lubbock, Texas, debated Anson Mount, religion editor of *Playboy* magazine, before 2000 Texas Tech students in the Lubbock municipal auditorium. Here are some quotable quotes by both men. The full text of the debate can be ordered from *Christian Chronicle*, Box 4055, Austin, Texas 78751. Cost: 25¢.

Quotes from Mr. Mount's opening statement:

"We are not advocates of irresponsible hedonism. We do not believe that people have a license to act without concern for others, for the welfare of themselves or others. We do not advocate pre-marital sex as the best possible kind of sex, as many people think we do. Not at all. We do not say casual sex is necessarily wrong. It may be wrong in most cases, and in the particular kind of hung-up society we live in, it often is. But it isn't by definition."

"We don't think there is anything wrong with enjoying life. As a matter of fact, people should. We don't think that people should enjoy life at the expense of others, however. That would be nothing but social anarchy."

"We believe that human welfare and happiness is the greatest good. Whatever promotes it, we are in favor of.

"The Christians believe in human welfare and happiness, too. And good for them. The humanists believe in human welfare and happiness, but for a different reason. The humanist believes that human welfare and happiness is an end in itself. Christians believe that because we love God, we must love our fellow man. And because we love our fellow man, we must seek his welfare and happiness. It's all the same thing. But this is the difference between humanism and Christianity. Christianity is supernatural, has its basis in a God—a personal God, an arbitrary God, a

---

*Mr. Banowsky became vice-president of Pepperdine College, Los Angeles, California in the fall of 1968.

God who lives up in the sky and presumably pulls strings. The humanist doesn't feel the need to believe in this."

"The churches emphasized some morals very strangely, and neglected others. It's really strange to see how this works. The churches—I'm not talking about Christianity, I'm talking about the churchmen—have emphasized sexual morality. Boy, have they been very, very rigid about that. They've emphasized drinking. Have they been very rigid about that!

"Now if I know my Christian theology, and I think I do, gluttony is just as serious a personal sin as any of the other possible intemperate indulgences. And I see dozens of fat ladies walking down the streets with no apparent guilt on their countenances. I've never been invited to Lubbock, Texas to take part in a Sunday morning discussion of eating morals.

"There are all kinds of very horrible things that come from overeating. Hypertension, heart disease, obesity. How many people dig their graves with their teeth? I haven't heard any sermons on the subject lately. It's strange how the church overlooks that.

"I know a 300-pound archbishop! But I've never heard anybody challenge his moral integrity."

"What about driving? Reckless driving is one of the most immoral things I can think of. But Jesus didn't say anything about reckless driving. He did say something about being concerned for your fellow man, which applies to driving, I suppose. But we overlook that. We really don't think of driving as an exercise in immorality, do we? But it is. Reckless driving is one of the most immoral things we can do. We are taking a chance on killing ourselves and our fellow man. But what about if you're taking a sick child to the hospital and you drive fast or go over the speed limit? That's a little different matter, isn't it?"

"The traditional legalistic approach to sex is inhuman very often—very inhuman. The thing that makes sex moral is not the fact that a preacher stands up in front of you and says some words. Sex can be vilely immoral within marriage. It can be coarse and demeaning and dehumanizing. For that same reason, it can be moral outside marriage.

"It's not the fact that a preacher stood in front of you that makes it moral. It's the quality of the relationship.

It's also true that if it's a good relationship, if it's a moral relationship, it's very likely going to end up in marriage."

Quotes from Mr. Banowsky's reply:

"It's true that a 300-pound bishop is immoral. It is also true that a man can drive his car immorally as well as love a woman immorally. But the Playboy empire has not been built upon center-page foldouts of cars.

"Neither, I would add, is the so-called Playboy philosophy a discourse on traffic techniques.

"The reason no Baptist preachers have written you letters because of the food you display in your magazine is because that's not on your menu."

"But among other things, the Playboy philosophy encourages extra-marital, pre-marital, and what Mr. Hefner has termed recreational sex . . ."

"The idea of extra-marital sex is not new. What is new, and I suppose this is what has disturbed me most, is the incredible but quite serious public campaign of Playboy philosophy to promote non-marital sexual intercourse as a Christian way of life. As scandalous as it may sound, I think Mr. Hefner is a man of conviction on this point."

"Christ's call to men was, 'whosoever would be truly great needs to become the servant of men.'

"Mr. Hefner's gospel proclaims 'we oppose the tendency to selflessness in our society.'

"What he affirms is a hedonism. While Anson says he is not for irresponsible hedonism, and so we'll not accuse him of that, he is for hedonism, which by definition means that pleasure is the greatest good in life. Sensual gratification, therefore, is to be the moral law by which one seeks pleasure fulfillment.

"Mr. Hefner tends to promote a kind of enlightened self-interest, which ends up being the most crass form of egoism. The apex of his selfishness in his sermon that women exist for the sole purpose of the pleasure of men, and that they exist for the purpose of allowing a man at any time or place to seduce any consenting female when his urge arises."

"It comes down to this: in all the universe, people are ultimate and people are to be loved, never used. Only things are to be used. The greatest immorality is to love things and use people, especially to use people as things.

"While Mr. Mount maintains that casual sex need not be wholly selfish, he is extremely naive if he fails to know that extra-marital sex is simply the giving of self, with reservation, the giving of body without the legal commitment, the giving of body without the vows for better or for worse, the giving of body without the giving of one's total self."

"When a man makes of sex a plaything, he forfeits the real thing."

"Or as Dr. Leslie H. Farber, a distinguished Washington psychoanalyst, has pointed out, 'The logical conclusion of hedonism, the use of sex for purely personal private pleasure, and apart from the context of humanity, is masturbation.'"

GLOSSARY

Key Terms Used in "It All Depends"

Abortion—the act of artificially relieving the pregnant uterus (womb) of its contents; causing an embryo or fetus to be separated from the uterus.

Absolutism—the ethical approach to right and wrong that says there is but one eternally true and valid moral code and this moral code applies impartially to all men.

Adultery—the voluntary, illicit sexual intercourse between a married person and a person of the opposite sex who is not the lawful spouse.

Agape—divine love, sacrificial, undying; in its deepest sense *agape* is the spontaneous result of a vital relationship with God who is *agape*.

Antinomian—one who disregards laws, literally "against law"; one who holds all rules and laws as no moral obligation.

Biblical morality—the morality taught by Scripture alone; not to be confused with the "old morality," which is based on religious rules, codes and traditions. Biblical morality is the foundation of Christian ethics.

Chastity—the quality or state of being innocent of unlawful sexual intercourse—premarital intercourse or extramarital intercourse (adultery).

230

Christian ethics—a view of right and wrong based on the principles of Scripture and the teachings of Christ.

Contraceptive—a device, chemical, or pill to prevent conception; a means of preventing the male sperm from fertilizing the female egg.

Embryo—in humans, the developing fertilized egg between the time of conception and eight weeks of age; after eight weeks, the embryo becomes a fetus.

Epicureanism—a philosophy following the ideas of Epicurus, ancient Greek philosopher who taught a form of hedonism that advocated a simple life of meditation; often confused with the "eat, drink and be merry" point of view.

Ethics—the science of moral values and duties; the science of discovering one's moral duty and obligation, the study of good and bad.

Extramarital sex—any sexual act outside of marriage; fornication or adultery.

Fornication—sexual intercourse on the part of an unmarried person.

Free love—sex with no laws or moral restraints of any kind.

"Going all the way"—popular terminology for extending petting into sexual intercourse.

Hedonism—a system of ethics teaching that pleasure or happiness is the sole or chief good in life.

Homosexual—a person who has sexual desire or love for one of his or her own sex.

Immorality—breaking of moral codes, laws or principles; direct disobedience of what you know to be good and right.

Intercourse (sexual)—penetration of the vagina by the penis with the emission of seminal fluid by the male; also known as coitus.

Incest—sexual intercourse between persons of close relationship.

Lesbian—the name for the homosexual female; lesbianism refers specifically to any abnormal attachment or excessive affection between two women.

Legalism—a system of morals and ethics based on strict obedience to rules, regulations and laws established by Biblical principles, parents or other authorities.

Love—warm affection, attachment and devotion to another person. Three common "love" relationships are: *philia*, refers to the love of companionship; *eros*, refers to love in a sexual setting; *agape*, refers to the sacrificial, undying love of God, God's love reflected in those who have a close relationship with Him.

231

Marriage—in our society, a life-long commitment of a man and woman to each other; includes the full privilege of sharing and enjoying sex.

Masturbation—self-production of an orgasm by exciting the genital organs; sex by yourself.

Moral—that which is recognized as right and good.

Morality—a doctrine or system of moral duties; the quality of an action as estimated by a standard of right and wrong.

Necking—sex play, involving closeness, kissing, touching—"from the neck up."

Neighbor—commonly used to designate one who lives near another; in terms of Christian ethics, anyone with whom your life comes in contact—actually, any other person.

New morality—an ethical system that does not depend on traditions and set standards, but places the responsibility for behavior on the individual's decision of "What is right for me—now?"

Old morality—an ethical system that depends on the guidance of a set religious or moral code, the authority of laws, parental or Biblical commandments.

Orgasm—the climax of the sexual act; a pleasurable experience for the female and male, accompanied by seminal emission by the male.

Petting—sex play, commonly used to refer to nearness, kissing, caressing, "from the neck down."

Pregnancy—the nine-month period, from fertilization until birth, that the mother carries the growing baby in her uterus.

Premarital sex—sexual intercourse before marriage.

Promiscuity—unrestricted sexual relations with no regard to life-long commitment.

Pharisaism—rigid observance of rites and forms of religion without sincerity or true devotion.

Pornography—indecent or offensive writing, pictures, jokes; term used to refer to "girlie" publications, obscene pictures and the like.

Prostitute—a girl or woman who engages in sexual intercourse for payment. Also called a harlot or whore.

Puritanism—a highly restrictive moral code that emphasized the repression of pleasures; considered sex as a necessary evil to be endured for the sake of procreation, not a gift of God to be enjoyed.

Rape—the criminal act of forcing a female into sex relations against her will; sexual attack or assault upon the female.

Relativism—the view that holds there is no absolute but

that right and wrong is dependent on and determined by
its relationship to a situation.

Sex—the instinctive drive that attracts man to woman,
woman to man and insures the continuation of mankind.

Sexuality—the total meaning of being a man and the total
meaning of being a woman; sexuality is more than sex, it
is the entire role of being a male, from little boy to grown
man; it is the entire role of being a female, from little girl
to mature woman.

Situation ethics—a system of ethics that recognizes only one
law—the law of love; requires the individual to know what
is the "loving thing to do" in each situation and to decide
for himself what is right.

Summary commandment—Christ's summary statement of the
Ten Commandments in Matt. 22:35-40.

Venereal disease—an infection transmitted through sexual
intercourse, such as syphilis and gonorrhea; commonly
known as VD.

Victorianism—a stilted, prim view of life that emphasized
modesty to the point of being ridiculous; held that sex was
not to be mentioned and should be avoided as much as
possible.

FOR FURTHER READING

If you want to know more about ethics,
deciding between right and wrong. . .

Right or Wrong, T. B. Maston. Broadman Press, 1955.
Get Off the Fence! Thomas A. Fry, Jr. Fleming H. Revell,
1963.
And None Would Believe It, M. Basilea Schlink. Zonder-
van, 1967.
Fractured Questions, Warren Mild. The Judson Press, 1966.
"It's My Life, Isn't It?" Condensed from *Christian Herald*.
Reader's Digest, October, 1968.

If you want to know about sex . . . the "facts of life,"
masturbation, homosexuality . .

Of Sex and Saints, Donald F. Tweedie, Jr. Baker Book
House, 1965.
Love and the Facts of Life, Evelyn Duvall. Association
Press, 1963.
Life Can Be Sexual, Elmer N. Witt. Concordia Publishing
House, 1967.

Sense and Nonsense About Sex, Evelyn and Sylvanus Duvall. Association Press, 1962.
The Stork Didn't Bring You, Lois Pemberton. Thomas Nelson and Sons, 1965.

If you want to know about venereal disease . . .

Some Questions and Answers About VD. Pamphlet available from the American Social Health Association, 1790 Broadway, New York, N. Y. 5 cents each.
What You Should Know About VD—and Why, Bruce Webster, M. D. Available from Scholastic Book Service, 50 West 44th Street, New York, N. Y. 10036.
Teen-Agers and Venereal Disease, Celia S. Deschin. Department of Health, Education and Welfare, Public Health Service, 1961.

If you want to know, "why wait until marriage?" . . .

Why Wait Till Marriage? Evelyn Duvall. Association Press, 1965.
Love and the Facts of Life, Evelyn Millis Duvall. Association Press, 1963. See Part One, "Your Love Feelings," pp. 14-74.
Sense and Nonsense About Sex, Evelyn and Sylvanus Duvall. Association Press, 1962. See Chapter 5, "Love is Not the Same as Sex," pp. 72-89.
I Loved a Girl, Walter Trobisch. Harper Chapel Books, Harper and Row, 1965.
"Teen Love, Teen Marriage," by the Public Affairs Committee. Grossett and Dunlap, 1966.
"Teen-Age Marriage—Yes or No?" Condensed from *Seventeen.* Anonymous. *Reader's Digest*, November, 1968.
The Art of Dating, Evelyn Millis Duvall. Association Press, 1958.

If you want to know about preparing for marriage . . .

Letters to Karen, Charlie W. Shedd. Abingdon Press, 1965.
Letters to Phillip: On How to Treat a Woman, Charlie W. Shedd. Doubleday, 1968.
Toward Christian Marriage, W. Melville Capper and H. Morgan William. Inter-Varsity Press, 1958.
Dear Abby on Marriage, Abigail Van Buren. McGraw-Hill Book Co., 1962.
Design for Christian Marriage, Dwight H. Small. Fleming H. Revell, 1959.
To Live in Love, Eileen Guder. Zondervan, 1967.
Make Love Your Aim, Eugenia Price. Zondervan, 1967.